Schweser Weekly Class Workbook
2015 CFA Level I

Volume 1

KAPLAN

SCHWESER

SCHWESER WEEKLY CLASS WORKBOOK: 2015 CFA LEVEL I,
VOLUME 1
©2014 Kaplan, Inc. All rights reserved.

Published in December 2014 by Kaplan Schweser.
Printed in the United States of America.

ISBN: 978-1-4754-2766-0 / 1-4754-2766-2

PPN: 3200-5539

Contents

Study Session 2

Quantitative Methods: Basic Concepts

Quantitative Methods

Quantitative Methods: Basic Concepts

5. The Time Value of Money

KAPLAN UNIVERSITY SCHOOL OF PROFESSIONAL AND CONTINUING EDUCATION | SCHWESER

Quantitative Methods

Study Session 2
Quantitative Methods: Basic Concepts

5. The Time Value of Money
6. Discounted Cash Flow Applications
7. Statistical Concepts and Market Returns
8. Probability Concepts

KAPLAN UNIVERSITY SCHOOL OF PROFESSIONAL AND CONTINUING EDUCATION | SCHWESER

The Time Value of Money

LOS 5.c Calculate/Interpret
CFAI p. 287, Schweser p. 105

A CD has an effective annual yield of 4.2%.

1. What is its stated annual rate if compounding is **quarterly?**

2. What is the stated annual rate if compounding is **monthly?**

© Kaplan, Inc.   3 – 3

The Time Value of Money

LOS 5.c Calculate/Interpret
CFAI p. 287, Schweser p. 105

$100,000 CD has a stated annual rate of 3.6%.

1. What is the effective annual yield (EAY) if compounding is **quarterly?**

2. What is the EAY if compounding is **monthly?**

© Kaplan, Inc.   2 – 3

LOS 5.d Solve
CFAI p. 284, Schweser p. 107   The Time Value of Money

Compounding and Future Value

An investor puts $1,000 into an account that has a stated rate of 10% per year and takes no money out:

How much will be in the account after 4 years if compounding is <u>annual</u>?

$$1,000 \times 1.1^4 = 1,464.10$$

How much will be in the account after 4 years if compounding is <u>quarterly</u>?

$$1,000 \times \left(1+ \frac{0.10}{4}\right)^{(4 \times 4)} = 1,000 \times 1.025^{16} = \$1,484.51$$

© Kaplan, Inc.   5

LOS 5.d Solve
CFAI p. 284, Schweser p. 107   The Time Value of Money

What is the monthly payment on a $100,000, 30-year home loan with a stated rate of 6%?

© Kaplan, Inc.   4 - 5

The Time Value of Money

A preferred stock will pay $8 per year forever, and the rate of return is 10%. What is its present value?

© Kaplan, Inc.   7 - 2

LOS 5.e,f Calculate/Interpret/Demonstrate
CFAI p. 280, Schweser p. 108   The Time Value of Money

Discounting and Present Value

What is the present value of $1,000 to be received in two years when the interest rate is 10%

I = 10%

| 0 | 1 | 2 | 3 |

PV ← $1,000

N = 2; I/Y = 10; FV = –1,000; PMT = 0; CPT → PV = $826.45

$$PV = \frac{FV}{(1+i)^n} \qquad \frac{1,000}{1.1^2} = \$826.45$$

© Kaplan, Inc.   6 - 2

PV of an Ordinary Annuity

What is the present value of $200 to be received at the end of each year for three years when the interest rate is 10%?

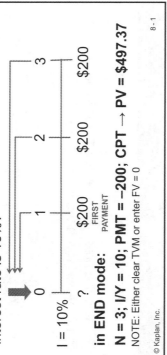

in END mode:

N = 3; I/Y = 10; PMT = –200; CPT → PV = $497.37

NOTE: Either clear TVM or enter FV = 0

© Kaplan, Inc.

8-1

FV of an Ordinary Annuity

What is the value in three years of $200 to be received at the end of each year for three years when the interest rate is 10%?

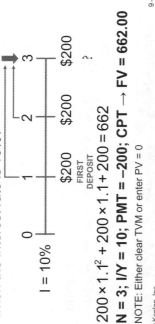

$$200 \times 1.1^2 + 200 \times 1.1 + 200 = 662$$

N = 3; I/Y = 10; PMT = –200; CPT → FV = 662.00

NOTE: Either clear TVM or enter PV = 0

© Kaplan, Inc.

9-2

PV of an Annuity Due

What is the present value of $200 to be received at the start of each year for three years when the interest rate is 10%?

Annuity Due: CFs at the beginning of each period

$$200 + 200 / 1.1 + 200 / 1.1^2 = \$547.11$$

Calculator, in BGN mode

N = 3; I/Y = 10; PMT = –200; FV = 0; CPT→PV = $547.11

© Kaplan, Inc.

10-2

FV of an Annuity Due

An investor deposits $200 at the beginning of each year for three years into an account that yields 10%. What is the value of the account at the end of the third year?

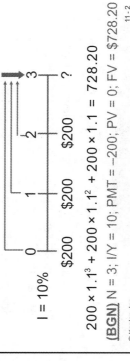

$$200 \times 1.1^3 + 200 \times 1.1^2 + 200 \times 1.1 = 728.20$$

(BGN) N = 3; I/Y = 10; PMT = –200; PV = 0; FV = $728.20

© Kaplan, Inc.

11-2

LOS 5.e,f Calculate/Interpret/Demonstrate
CFAI p. 280, Schweser p. 108   The Time Value of Money

Deferred Annuity

What is the present value of an annuity of three payments of $200 each that begins five periods from now if the discount rate is 10%?

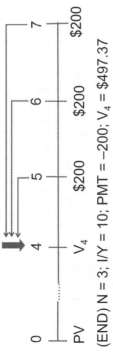

0	4	5	6	7
	V_4	$200	$200	$200

PV

(END) N = 3; I/Y = 10; PMT = −200; V_4 = $497.37

PV = 497.37/1.1^4 = $339.71

© Kaplan, Inc.   12 - 1

LOS 5.e,f Calculate/Interpret/Demonstrate
CFAI p. 280, Schweser p. 108   The Time Value of Money

Elmer has won his $4 million state lottery and has been offered 20 annual payments of $200,000 each beginning today or a single payment of $2,267,000. What is the annual discount rate used to calculate the lump-sum payout amount?

© Kaplan, Inc.   13 - 1

The Time Value of Money

Elmer borrows $100,000 at 9% and will make annual end-of-year payments of $13,966. How many payments must Elmer make to pay off the loan?

© Kaplan, Inc.   14 - 1

LOS 5.f Demonstrate
CFAI p. 281, Schweser p. 123   The Time Value of Money

A client has $75,000 in savings now, will retire 20 years from today, and needs 25 payments of $62,000/year to begin then. Account is expected to earn 7%/year.

1. How much is needed at T = 20 to fund retirement?

2. What annual deposit must she make at the end of each year for 20 years to reach her goal?

© Kaplan, Inc.   15 - 4

You are analyzing the last five years of earnings per share data for a company. The figures are $4.00, $4.50, $5.00, $6.00, and $7.00. At what compound annual rate did EPS grow during these years?

[END mode] N = 24, FV = 0, PMT = –62,000, I/Y = 7,
CPT   1,099 + 62,000 = $773,099

16 – 1

Additional Learning Outcomes

LOS 5.a: interpreting interest rates

LOS 5.b: risk premiums and nominal interest rates

[END mode] N = 24, FV = 0, PMT = –62,000, I/Y = 7,
CPT   1,099 + 62,000 = $773,099

17

Quantitative Methods: Basic Concepts

6. Discounted Cash Flow Applications

Net Present Value (NPV)

The sum of the present values of a series of cash flows

$$NPV = CF_0 + \frac{CF_1}{(1+k)^1} + \frac{CF_2}{(1+k)^2} + \cdots + \frac{CF_n}{(1+k)^n}$$

19

LOS 6.a Calculate/Interpret
CFAI p. 332, Schweser p. 143   Discounted Cash Flow Applications

Net Present Value (NPV)

Example using a 9% discount rate

End of Year	Project X	Discounted Cash Flow
0	–$100	–$100.00
1	25	22.94
2	50	42.08
3	75	57.91
		NPV = $22.93

NPV is the change in wealth in present value terms from a series of cash flows

© Kaplan, Inc.   20

LOS 6.a Calculate/Interpret
CFAI p. 332, Schweser p. 143   Discounted Cash Flow Applications

What is the NPV with a discount rate of 10% of the following cash flows?

Initial outlay: $-100,000

End of years 1,2, and 3: $30,000

End of years 4 and 5: 25,000

© Kaplan, Inc.   21-1

LOS 6.a Calculate/Interpret
CFAI p. 332, Schweser p. 143   Discounted Cash Flow Applications

Internal Rate of Return (IRR)

IRR is the discount rate that equates the PV of a series of cash flows to their cost

The IRR is the discount rate that makes the NPV = 0

$$NPV = 0 = CF_0 + \frac{CF_1}{(1+IRR)^1} + \frac{CF_2}{(1+IRR)^2} + \cdots + \frac{CF_n}{(1+IRR)^n}$$

© Kaplan, Inc.   22

LOS 6.a Calculate/Interpret
CFAI p. 332, Schweser p. 143   Discounted Cash Flow Applications

Internal Rate of Return (IRR)

End of Year	Project X CFs	Discounted Cash Flow at 19.4%
0	–$100	–100.00
1	$25	+20.94
2	$50	+35.07
3	$75	+44.06

$\Sigma = 0.00 = NPV$

Because NPV = 0
IRR = 19.4%

CPT IRR with CF function

© Kaplan, Inc.   23

| Discounted Cash Flow Applications |

What is the IRR of an investment today of $100,000 that will make the following cash flows?

End of years 1, 2, and 3: $30,000

End of years 4 and 5: $25,000

24 - 1

© Kaplan, Inc.

LOS 6.b Contrast
CFAI p. 336, Schweser p. 146 | Discounted Cash Flow Applications |

Possible Problems With IRR

1. When a series of cash flows has more than one change of sign, there can be more than one IRR

2. Comparing two projects, one can have higher NPV while the other has higher IRR

More on NPV and IRR in Corporate Finance

25

© Kaplan, Inc.

LOS 6.c Calculate/Interpret
CFAI p. 339, Schweser p. 148 | Discounted Cash Flow Applications |

Holding Period Return (HPR)

The percentage increase in wealth over a period

1. Investment purchased nine months ago for $9 is now valued at $10.20. What is the holding period return?

9-month HPR is 10.20 / 9 − 1 = 1.20 / 9 = 13.33%

2. Stock purchased one year ago for $29 just paid a dividend of $1.30 and is valued at $30.50. What is the holding period (total) return?

(30.50 + 1.30) / 29 − 1 = 9.66%

26 - 2

© Kaplan, Inc.

| Discounted Cash Flow Applications |

An investor buys a stock for $20/sh. and sells it 9 months later for $22.50.

1. What is the (9-month) holding period yield?

2. What is the effective annual yield?

27 - 2

© Kaplan, Inc.

Discounted Cash Flow Applications

An investor buys a stock for $20/sh. and sells it 18 months later for $24 after collecting $1.10 in dividends.

1. What is the holding period total return?

25.50%

2. What is the effective annual return?

~~KNOCK~~ 16.3%

LOS 6.d Calculate/Compare/Evaluate
CFAI p. 340, Schweser p. 148   Discounted Cash Flow Applications

Time-Weighted Returns

Annual time-weighted returns are effective annual compound returns.

$$TWR = \left[\left(\frac{End\ Value_1}{Begin\ Value_1}\right)\left(\frac{End\ Value_2}{Begin\ Value_2}\right)\cdots\left(\frac{End\ Value_N}{Begin\ Value_N}\right)\right]^{\frac{1}{\#YEARS}} - 1$$

Periods can be any length

Calculate HPRs for periods between significant cash flows

$1 + HPR_1$

LOS 6.d Calculate/Compare/Evaluate
CFAI p. 340, Schweser p. 148   Discounted Cash Flow Applications

Money-Weighted Returns

Money-weighted returns are like an IRR measure

$$CF_0 + \frac{CF_1}{1+MWR} + \cdots + \frac{CF_N}{(1+MWR)^N} = 0$$

Periods must be equal length, use shortest period with no significant cash flows

---

Reference Level I CFA Curriculum,
Reading 6, Problem 6   Discounted Cash Flow Applications

Jan.1, 20X1: buys 150 sh. ABM for $156.30.

Jan.1, 20X2: receives dividend of $10/sh., sells 100 sh. for $165/sh., does not reinvest dividends.

Jan.1, 20X3: receives dividend of $15/sh., sells remaining 50 sh. for $170.

What is the investor's annual time-weighted return?

12.04%

Jan.1, 20X1: buys 150 sh. ABM for $156.30.

Jan.1, 20X2: receives dividend of $10/sh., sells 100 sh. for $165/sh., does not reinvest dividends.

Jan.1, 20X3: receives dividend of $15/sh., sells remaining 50 sh. for $170.

What is the investor's annual money-weighted return?

12.9%

© Kaplan, Inc.   32 - 2

BDY, HPY, EAY, MMY

Bank discount yield $= \dfrac{\text{Discount}}{\text{Face}} \times \dfrac{360}{\text{days to maturity}}$

Holding period yield $= \dfrac{\text{Ending value}}{\text{Beginning value}} - 1$

Effective annual yield $= (1 + HPY)^{\frac{365}{\text{days}}} - 1$

Money market yield $= HPY \times \dfrac{360}{\text{days to maturity}}$

© Kaplan, Inc.   33

Yields for 90-day t-bill Priced at $980

$BDY = \dfrac{20}{1,000} \times \dfrac{360}{90} = 8\%$ — Simple annualized discount

$HPY = \dfrac{1,000}{980} - 1 = 2.04\%$ — 90-day HPY

$EAY = (1.0204)^{\frac{365}{90}} - 1 = 8.53\%$ — Effective rate

$MMY = 0.0204 \times \dfrac{360}{90} = 8.16\%$ — Simple annualized

© Kaplan, Inc.   34

A 90-day T-bill is purchased for $997.40. What are the discount yield, holding period yield, money market yield, and the effective yield?

Discount yield: 1.04%

90-day HPY: 0.2603%

Money market yield: 1.0428

Effective annual yield: 1.0614

© Kaplan, Inc.   35 - 4

Quantitative Methods

Quantitative Methods: Basic Concepts

7. Statistical Concepts and Market Returns

KAPLAN UNIVERSITY SCHOOL OF PROFESSIONAL AND CONTINUING EDUCATION | SCHWESER

Converting Between Yield Measures

A money market security with 173 days to maturity has a money market yield of 4.53%, what is its effective annual yield?

$$MMY = HPY \times \frac{360}{\text{days to maturity}}, \quad HPY = MMY \times \frac{\text{days to maturity}}{360}$$

$$HPY = 4.53\% \times \frac{173}{360} = 2.177\%$$

$$EAY = (1 + HPY)^{\frac{365}{\text{days}}} - 1, \quad EAY = (1 + 0.02177)^{\frac{365}{173}} - 1 = 4.649\%$$

© Kaplan, Inc.   36

Describing a Statistical Distribution

- A relative frequency distribution shows the percentage of a distribution's outcomes in each interval
- A cumulative frequency distribution shows the percentage of observations less than the upper bound of each interval

© Kaplan, Inc.   39

Describing Data or Distribution

Measures of central tendency
- Mean (arithmetic, geometric, harmonic)
- Median, ½ higher and ½ lower
- Mode, most frequent outcome

Measures of dispersion
- Standard deviation, variance
- Range, highest to lowest
- MAD, mean absolute deviation

© Kaplan, Inc.   38

LOS 7.d Describe
CFAI p. 373, Schweser p. 174

Histogram

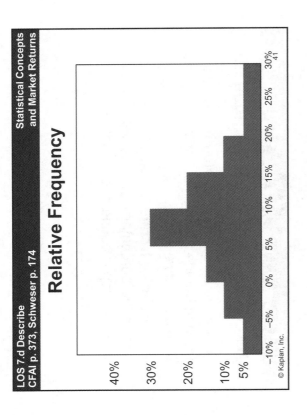

© Kaplan, Inc.

LOS 7.d Describe
CFAI p. 373, Schweser p. 174

Relative Frequency

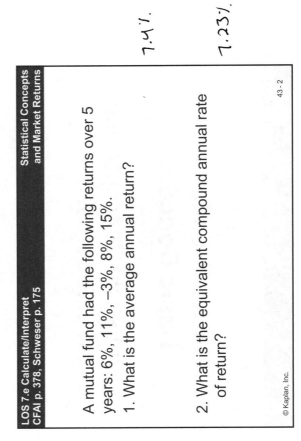

© Kaplan, Inc.

LOS 7.d Describe
CFAI p. 373, Schweser p. 174

Cumulative Relative Frequency

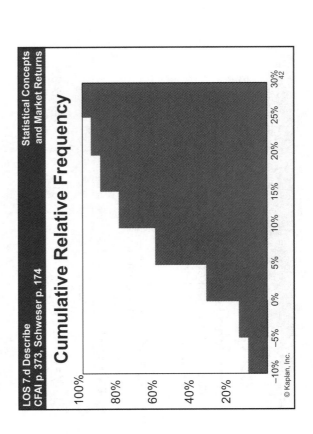

© Kaplan, Inc.

LOS 7.e Calculate/Interpret
CFAI p. 378, Schweser p. 175

A mutual fund had the following returns over 5 years: 6%, 11%, −3%, 8%, 15%.

1. What is the average annual return?

7.4%.

2. What is the equivalent compound annual rate of return?

7.23%.

© Kaplan, Inc.

43 - 2

LOS 7.e Calculate/Interpret
CFAI p. 378, Schweser p. 175

Statistical Concepts and Market Returns

Asset allocation in an investment account:
Cash 10%, Stock 35%, Bonds 55%

Annual returns:
Cash = 2%, Stock = 16%, Bonds 8%

What is the account return for the year?

(handwritten) 10.4%

© Kaplan, Inc.

44 - 1

LOS 7.e Calculate/Interpret
CFAI p. 378, Schweser p. 175

Statistical Concepts and Market Returns

(handwritten) 23.22

Investor buys $3,000 of a stock at the end of Month 1 at $20 a share, and $3,000 at the end of Month 2 at $25 per share.

What is the average cost per share of stock?

© Kaplan, Inc.

45 - 1

LOS 7.e Calculate/Interpret
CFAI p. 378, Schweser p. 175

Statistical Concepts and Market Returns

Comparing Means

Calculate the arithmetic, geometric, and harmonic means of 2, 3, and 4.

Arithmetic: $\dfrac{2+3+4}{3} = 3$

Largest

Geometric: $\sqrt[3]{2 \times 3 \times 4} = 2.88$

Harmonic: $\dfrac{3}{\frac{1}{2} + \frac{1}{3} + \frac{1}{4}} = 2.77$

Smallest

© Kaplan, Inc.

46 - 4

LOS 7.e Calculate/Interpret
CFAI p. 378, Schweser p. 175

Statistical Concepts and Market Returns

Median

- Midpoint of a data set, **half above and half below**
- With an odd number of observations

  2, 5, 7, 11, 14   Median = 7

- With an even number of observations, median is the average of the two middle observations

  3, 9, 10, 20   Median = (9 + 10) / 2 = 9.5

Less affected by extreme values than the mean

© Kaplan, Inc.

47

Slide 48

Mode

Value occurring most frequently in a data set

2, 4, 5, 5, 7, *8, 8, 8*, 10, 12   Mode = 8

- Data sets can have more than one mode (bimodal, trimodal, etc.)

© Kaplan, Inc.

48

Slide 49

Quantiles

75% of the data points are less than the 3rd **quartile**

60% of the data points are less than the 60th **percentile** (6th decile)

$$\text{Percentile position}_y = (n+1)\frac{y}{100}$$

−3   0   5   5   7   11   17   18   20   23   29

With 11 observations, the 70th **percentile** position is **(11 + 1) × 0.70 = 8.4**; 18 + 0.4(20 − 18) = 18.8

© Kaplan, Inc.

49

Slide 50-2

Given annual returns data: 15%, −5%, 12%, 22%

1. What is the data's Range?

2. What is the data's Mean Absolute Deviation?

© Kaplan, Inc.

50 - 2

Slide 51

Population Variance and Standard Deviation

Variance is the average of the squared deviations from the mean

Standard deviation is the square root of variance

$$\sigma^2 = \frac{\sum_{i=1}^{N}(X_i - \mu)^2}{N} \qquad \sigma = \sqrt{\sigma^2}$$

© Kaplan, Inc.

51

LOS 7.g Calculate/Interpret
CFAI p. 402, Schweser p. 181

Statistical Concepts and Market Returns

Sample Variance (s²) and Sample Standard Deviation (s)

$$s^2 = \frac{\sum_{i=1}^{n}\left(x_i - \overline{x}\right)^2}{n-1} \qquad s = \sqrt{\frac{\sum_{i=1}^{n}\left(x_i - \overline{x}\right)^2}{n-1}}$$

Note that for sample variance, the sum of the squared deviations is **divided by n – 1 instead of *n***

© Kaplan, Inc.

52

LOS 7.g Calculate/Interpret
CFAI p. 402, Schweser p. 181

Statistical Concepts and Market Returns

Calculating Variance (σ²)

Returns on four stocks are 15%, –5%, 12%, and 22%. What are the population and sample standard deviation?

Population Mean (μ) = 11%

$$\sigma^2 = \frac{(15-11)^2 + (-5-11)^2 + (12-11)^2 + (22-11)^2}{4} = 98.5$$

$$\sigma = 9.9\%$$

$$s^2 = \frac{(15-11)^2 + (-5-11)^2 + (12-11)^2 + (22-11)^2}{3} = 131.3$$

$$s_x = 11.5\%$$

© Kaplan, Inc.

53 - 8

LOS 7.h Calculate/Interpret
CFAI p. 412, Schweser p. 185

Statistical Concepts and Market Returns

Chebyshev's Inequality

Specifies the **minimum percentage** of observations that lie within *k* standard deviations of the mean; applies to any distribution with k > 1

$$\boxed{\text{Min. \% is } 1 - \frac{1}{k^2}}$$

Min. % for 2 std. dev. is $1 - \frac{1}{2^2} = 1 - \frac{1}{4} = 75\%$

© Kaplan, Inc.

54

LOS 7.i Calculate/Interpret
CFAI p. 414, Schweser p. 186

Statistical Concepts and Market Returns

Coefficient of Variation (CV)

A measure of risk per unit of return

Example:	Mean	Std. Dev.
Asset A	5%	10%
Asset B	8%	12%

Asset B has higher std. dev. and higher return

Lower CV is better, less risk per unit of return

$$CV = \frac{s}{\overline{X}} \qquad CV_A = \frac{10}{5} = 2 \qquad CV_B = \frac{12}{8} = 1.5$$

© Kaplan, Inc.

55

Sharpe Ratio

Excess return per unit of risk (CV measures risk per unit of return); **higher is better**

Mean portfolio return = 17%, standard deviation = 9%, average risk-free rate = 5%.

What is the Sharpe ratio for the portfolio?

$$\text{Sharpe ratio} = \frac{\overline{R}_P - \overline{R}_F}{\sigma_P} = \frac{17-5}{9} = 1.33$$

Sharpe Ratio is Safety-first with R_f for target return

© Kaplan, Inc.

56

Rf = 4%	Port A	Port B	Port C
Return	8%	13%	17%
Std. Dev.	5%	9%	11%

1. Which portfolio is preferred based on their CV?

2. Which portfolio is preferred based on their Sharpe ratios?

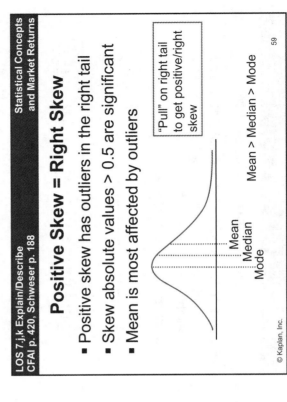

© Kaplan, Inc.

57 - 2

Skewness

- Skew measures the degree to which a distribution lacks symmetry
- A symmetrical distribution has skew = 0

Symmetrical.
Mean = Median = Mode

Mean
Median
Mode

© Kaplan, Inc.

58

Positive Skew = Right Skew

- Positive skew has outliers in the right tail
- Skew absolute values > 0.5 are significant
- Mean is most affected by outliers

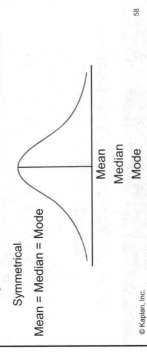

"Pull" on right tail to get positive/right skew

Mean
Median
Mode

Mean > Median > Mode

© Kaplan, Inc.

59

Slide 60

Negative Skew = Left Skew

- Negative skew has outliers in the left tail
- Mean is most affected by outliers
  "Median is in the middle"

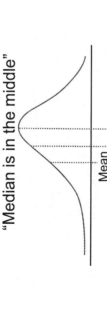

Mean < Median < Mode

© Kaplan, Inc.

60

Slide 61

Kurtosis

- Measures the degree to which a distribution is more or less peaked than a normal distribution
- *Leptokurtic* (kurtosis > 3) is **more peaked** with **fatter tails** (more extreme outliers)

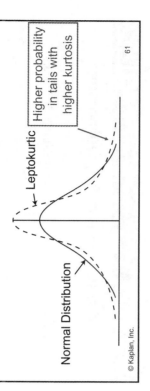

Higher probability in tails with higher kurtosis

Leptokurtic

Normal Distribution

© Kaplan, Inc.

61

Slide 62

Kurtosis

Kurtosis for a normal distribution is 3.0

Excess kurtosis is kurtosis minus 3

Excess kurtosis is *0 for a normal distribution*

Excess kurtosis greater than 1.0 in absolute value is considered significant

© Kaplan, Inc.

62

Slide 63

Arithmetic vs. Geometric Mean

Arithmetic mean annual return is expectation (best guess) of returns for any single year.

Geometric mean is estimate of average annual compound returns over multiple periods.

© Kaplan, Inc.

63

CFA Curriculum Vol. 1, R.7, Q.21, p. 440 — Statistical Concepts and Market Returns

Is a return distribution characterized by frequent small losses and a few large gains best described as having:

	negative skew?	a mean that is greater than the median?
A.	No	No
B.	No	Yes
C.	Yes	No

64 - 1

Reference Level I CFA Curriculum, Reading 7, Problem 22 — Statistical Concepts and Market Returns

	Skewness	Kurtosis
Portfolio A	–1.3	2.2
Portfolio B	0.5	3.5

Evaluate the following statements:

1. The distribution of Portfolio A is more peaked than a normal distribution.

2. The distribution for Portfolio B has a long tail on the left side.

© Kaplan, Inc.

65 - 4

Reference Level I CFA Curriculum, Reading 7, Problem 2 — Statistical Concepts and Market Returns

Identify the measurement scale of each data set.

A. Sales in euros.

B. The investment style of mutual funds.

C. An analyst's rating of *overweight, underweight,* and *market weight.*

D. Portfolio risk from 1(very conservative) to 5 (very risky), difference between 1 and 2 is the same increment in risk as the difference between 4 and 5.

© Kaplan, Inc.

66 - 4

Additional Learning Outcomes — Statistical Concepts and Market Returns

LOS 7.a: descriptive and inferential statistics, population vs. sample

LOS 7.b: parameters, sample statistics, and frequency distributions

© Kaplan, Inc.

67

LOS 8.b State/Distinguish
CFAI p. 459, Schweser p. 207

Probability Concepts

Two Properties of Probability

Probability of an event, $P(E_i)$, is between 0 and 1

$$0 \leq P(E_i) \leq 1$$

For a set of events that are mutually exclusive and exhaustive, the **sum of probabilities is 1**

$$\Sigma P(E_i) = 1$$

69

Quantitative Methods

Quantitative Methods: Basic Concepts

8. Probability Concepts

KAPLAN UNIVERSITY   SCHOOL OF PROFESSIONAL AND CONTINUING EDUCATION | SCHWESER

LOS 8.d Distinguish
CFAI p. 462, Schweser p. 209

Probability Concepts

Conditional vs. Unconditional

Two types of probability:

Unconditional: $P(A)$, the probability of an event regardless of the outcomes of other events (e.g., probability market will be up for the day)

Conditional: $P(A|B)$, the probability of A given that B has occurred (e.g., probability that the market will be up for the day, given that the Fed raises interest rates)

71

LOS 8.b State/Distinguish
CFAI p. 459, Schweser p. 207

Probability Concepts

Types of Probability

Empirical: Based on analysis of data

Subjective: Based on personal perception

A priori: Based on reasoning, not experience

70

Slide 72

LOS 8.e Explain
CFAI p. 463, Schweser p. 209

Probability Rules

Use **addition rule** for probability of A or B occurring

$P(A \text{ or } B) = P(A) + P(B) - P(AB)$

Use **multiplication rule** for joint probability

$Prob(AB) = Prob(A|B) \times Prob(B)$

Multiplication rule for independent probabilities

$Prob(AB) = Prob(A) \times Prob(B)$

For independence: $Prob(A|B) = Prob(A)$

© Kaplan, Inc.

72

Slide 73

LOS 8.e Explain
CFAI p. 463, Schweser p. 209

Probability Rules

Total probability rule

$Prob(A) = Prob(A|B) \times Prob(B)$
$\qquad + Prob(A|B^c) \times Prob(B^c)$

or

$Prob(A) = Prob(A|S_1) \times Prob(S_1)$
$\qquad + Prob(A|S_2) \times Prob(S_2)$
$\qquad + \ldots$
$\qquad + Prob(A|S_n) \times Prob(S_n)$

where $Prob(S_1) + Prob(S_2) + \ldots + Prob(S_n) = 1$

© Kaplan, Inc.

73

Slide 74

LOS 8.f Calculate/Interpret
CFAI p. 463, Schweser p. 210

Joint Probability

The probability that **both** of two events will occur is their **joint probability**

Example using conditional probability:

P (interest rates will increase) = P(I) = 40%

P (recession *given* a rate increase) = P(R|I) = 70%

Probability of a recession **and** an increase in rates,

$P(RI) = P(R|I) \times P(I) = 0.7 \times 0.4 = 28\%$

© Kaplan, Inc.

74

Slide 75

LOS 8.f Calculate/Interpret
CFAI p. 463, Schweser p. 210

Probability That at Least One of Two Events Will Occur

$P(A \text{ or } B) = P(A) + P(B) - P(AB)$

We must subtract the joint probability $P(AB)$

Don't double count P(AB)

P(A)   P(B)   P(AB)

© Kaplan, Inc.

75

LOS 8.f Calculate/Interpret
CFAI p. 463, Schweser p. 210   **Probability Concepts**

Addition Rule

P(I) = probability of rising interest rates is 40%

P(R) = probability of recession is 34%

Joint probability P(RI) = 0.28 (calculated earlier)

What is the probability of either rising interest rates **or** recession?

$$P(R \text{ or } I) = P(R) + P(I) - P(RI)$$
$$= 0.34 + 0.40 - 0.28 = 0.46$$

For mutually exclusive events, the
joint probability P(AB) = 0 so:
$$P(A \text{ or } B) = P(A) + P(B)$$

© Kaplan, Inc.   76 - 3

LOS 8.g Distinguish
CFAI p. 467, Schweser p. 213   **Probability Concepts**

Joint Probability of Any Number of Independent Events

Dependent events: Knowing the outcome of one tells you something about the probability of the other

Independent events: Occurrence of one event does not influence the occurrence of the other.

For the joint probability of independent events, just multiply

Example: Flipping a fair coin, P (heads) = 50%
The probability of 3 heads in succession is simply:
$0.5 \times 0.5 \times 0.5 = 0.5^3 = 0.125$, or 12.5%

© Kaplan, Inc.   77

LOS 8.h Calculate/Interpret
CFAI p. 469, Schweser p. 214   **Probability Concepts**

P (Interest rate increase) = P(I) = 40%

P (Recession | Increase) = P(R|I) = 0.70

P (Recession | No Increase) = P(R|I^c) = 0.10

What is the (unconditional) probability of recession?

© Kaplan, Inc.   78 - 1

Reference Level I CFA Curriculum,
Reading 8, Problem 19   **Probability Concepts**

Recovery of $100,000 defaulted loan

Scenario	Prob.	$Recovered	Prob.
#1	40%	50,000	60%
		30,000	40%
#2	60%	80,000	90%
		60,000	10%

Calculate the expected recovery amount.

© Kaplan, Inc.   79 - 1

LOS 8.i,j Explain
CFAI p. 474, Schweser p. 218

Expected Value, Conditional Expectations

Using the probabilities from the tree:

Expected(EPS) = $1.51
= 0.18(1.80) + 0.42(1.70) + 0.24(1.30) + 0.16(1.00)

Conditional expectations of EPS:

E(EPS)|GDP growth > 3% =
0.30(1.80) + 0.70(1.70) = $1.73

E(EPS)| GDP growth ≤ 3% =
0.60(1.30) + 0.40(1.00) = $1.18

© Kaplan, Inc.

81 - 2

LOS 8.i,j Explain
CFAI p. 474, Schweser p. 218

An Investment Tree

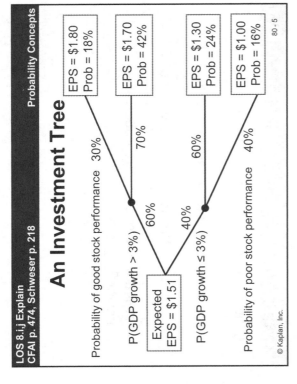

Probability of good stock performance 30%

EPS = $1.80
Prob = 18%

P(GDP growth > 3%)   70%

EPS = $1.70
Prob = 42%

60%

40%

Expected
EPS = $1.51

60%

P(GDP growth ≤ 3%)

EPS = $1.30
Prob = 24%

40%

EPS = $1.00
Prob = 16%

Probability of poor stock performance   40%

© Kaplan, Inc.

80 - 5

LOS 8.k Calculate/Interpret
CFAI p. 481, Schweser p. 219

Covariance

<u>Covariance</u>: A measure of how two variables move together

- Values range from minus infinity to plus infinity
- Units of covariance are difficult to interpret
- Covariance is positive when the two variables tend to be above (below) their expected values at the same time

For each observation, multiply each probability by the product of the two random variables' deviations from their means, and sum them

© Kaplan, Inc.

82

$Cov_{AB} = 0.0046$, $\sigma_A = 0.0623$, $\sigma_B = 0.0991$

What is the correlation between the two assets?

A. 0.633.

B. 0.745.

C. 0.812.

© Kaplan, Inc.

83 - 1

LOS 8.l Calculate/Interpret
CFAI p. 471, Schweser p. 223
Probability Concepts

Expected Value, Variance, and Standard Deviation (Probability Model)

Expected Value: $E(X) = \Sigma P(x_i)x_i$

Economy	$P(x_i)$	Return (x_i)	$P(x_i)x_i$
Recession	0.25	−0.10	−0.025
Normal	0.50	0.08	0.040
Boom	0.25	0.22	0.055
			$E(X) = 0.070$

© Kaplan, Inc.

84

LOS 8.l Calculate/Interpret
CFAI p. 471, Schweser p. 223
Probability Concepts

Expected Return, Variance, and Standard Deviation (Probability Model)

Variance: $\sigma^2{}_X = \Sigma P(x_i)[x_i - E(X)]^2$

Economy	$P(x_i)$	Return(x_i)	$P(x_i)x_i$	$P(x_i)[x_i-E(X)]^2$
Recession	0.25	−0.10	−0.025	0.00723
Normal	0.50	0.08	0.040	0.00005
Boom	0.25	0.22	0.055	0.00563
			$E(X) = 0.070$	$0.01290 = \sigma^2$

Standard deviation: Square root of $\sigma^2 = 0.1136$

© Kaplan, Inc.

85

LOS 8.l Calculate/Interpret
CFAI p. 471, Schweser p. 223
Probability Concepts

Portfolio Variance and Standard Deviation

Portfolio variance also uses the weights of the assets in the portfolio, use either formula

$$Var(R_p) = \sigma_A^2 w_A^2 + \sigma_B^2 w_B^2 + 2w_A w_B Cov_{AB}$$

Note: $Cov_{AB} = \rho_{AB}\sigma_A\sigma_B$

$$Var(R_p) = \sigma_A^2 w_A^2 + \sigma_B^2 w_B^2 + 2w_A w_B \rho_{AB}\sigma_A\sigma_B$$

Also covered in Portfolio Management

© Kaplan, Inc.

86

LOS 8.m Calculate/Interpret
CFAI p. 483, Schweser p. 224
Probability Concepts

Joint Probability Function

$E(R_B) = 18\%$

Returns	$R_B = 40\%$	$R_B = 20\%$	$R_B = 0\%$
$R_A = 20\%$	0.15		
$R_A = 15\%$		0.60	
$R_A = 4\%$			0.25

Probabilities

$E(R_A) = 13\%$

$Cov_{AB} = $ 0.15 $(0.20 - 0.13)$ $(0.40 - 0.18)$
  $+$ 0.6 $(0.15 - 0.13)$ $(0.20 - 0.18)$
  $+$ 0.25 $(0.04 - 0.13)$ $(0 - 0.18) = 0.0066$

© Kaplan, Inc.

87 - 2

Bayes' Formula

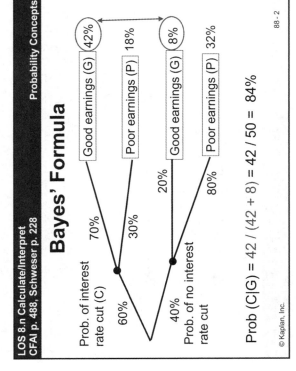

Prob. of interest
rate cut (C)   70%   Good earnings (G) 42%

                    30%   Poor earnings (P) 18%

60%

                    20%   Good earnings (G) 8%

40%   80%   Poor earnings (P) 32%
Prob. of no interest
rate cut

Prob (C|G) = 42 / (42 + 8) = 42 / 50 = 84%

88 - 2

© Kaplan, Inc.

Out of 10 stocks, 5 will be rated buy, 3 will be rated hold, and 2 will be rated sell. How many ways are there to do this?

A. 1,545.

B. 1,820.

C. 2,520.

89 - 1

© Kaplan, Inc.

Your firm intends to select 4 of 10 vice presidents for the investment committee. How many different groups of four are possible?

90 - 1

You have 5 stocks and want to sell 3, one at a time. How many ways are there to choose the 3 stocks to sell in order?

A. 10.

B. 30.

C. 60.

91 - 1

© Kaplan, Inc.

Additional Learning Outcomes

LOS 8.a: defining probability terms

LOS 8.c: odds for and against

92

© Kaplan, Inc.

Additional Problems

KAPLAN UNIVERSITY SCHOOL OF PROFESSIONAL AND CONTINUING EDUCATION | SCHWESER

Additional Problems

1) Key information about a two-asset portfolio is presented below:

Asset	Weight	Expected Return	Variance
J	0.60	15%	49
K	0.40	5%	36

Assets J and K have a correlation of 0.5714. What is this portfolio's variance?

A. 11.52.

B. 34.92.

C. 43.80.

- 3

© Kaplan, Inc.

Additional Problems

2) Consider the following probability distribution for a company's profit margin for next year:

Possible profit margin	Probability of profit margin
X	P(X)
−7%	0.10
−3%	0.50
4%	0.40

What is the variance of this probability distribution?

A. 3.93.

B. 15.44.

C. 41.49.

- 5

© Kaplan, Inc.

Additional Problems

4) Cliff Corporation's dividends the past six years were $0.31, $0.12, $0.40, $0.50, $0.60, and $0.70. The compound annual rate of dividend growth over this period is *closest* to:

A. 14.5%.

B. 17.7%.

C. 46.7%.

-2

© Kaplan, Inc.

Additional Problems

3) A 120-day Treasury bill has a money market yield of 3.25%. Its effective annual yield is *closest* to:

A. 3.28%.

B. 3.30%.

C. 3.33%.

-3

© Kaplan, Inc.

STUDY SESSION 2 ANSWERS

Reading	Slide Number	Answer
5	2(1)	3.649%
5	2(2)	3.66%
5	3(1)	4.136%
5	3(2)	4.1208%
5	4	−$599.5
5	7	$80
5	13	7%
5	14	N = 12
5	15(1)	$773,099
5	15(2)	$11,778.68
5	16	15.02%
6	21	$7,204
6	24	12.89%
6	27(1)	12.5%
6	27(2)	17%
6	28(1)	25.5%
6	28(2)	17%
6	31	12.04%
6	32	12.0%
6	35	1.04%, 0.2607%, 1.0428%, 1.0614%
7	43(1)	7.4%
7	43(2)	7.23%
7	44	10.2%
7	45	$22.22/sh.
7	50(1)	27%
7	50(2)	8%
7	57(1)	Portfolio A (CV=0.63)
7	57(2)	Portfolio C (Sharpe = 1.2)
7	64	B
7	65(1)	False
7	65(2)	False
7	66(A)	Ratio
7	66(B)	Nominal
7	66(C)	Ordinal
7	66(D)	Interval

Reading	Slide Number	Answer
8	78	0.34
8	79	$63,600
8	83	0.745
8	89	2,520
8	90	10
8	91	C

Additional Problems

1. B

2. B

3. C

4. B

Study Session 3

Quantitative Methods: Application

Quantitative Methods: Application

9. Common Probability Distributions

Study Session 3
Quantitative Methods: Application

9. Common Probability Distributions
10. Sampling and Estimation
11. Hypothesis Testing
12. Technical Analysis

Probability Functions

- The number of days next week on which it will rain is a discrete random variable that can take on the values {0,1,2,3,4,5,6,7}
- The amount of rain that will fall next week is a continuous random variable
- A probability function, $p(x)$, gives the probability that a discrete random variable will take on the value x

e.g., $p(x) = x / 15$ for $X = \{1,2,3,4,5\}$
→ $p(3) = 20\%$

Discrete and Continuous Probability Distributions

- A probability distribution gives the probabilities of all possible outcomes for a random variable
- A discrete distribution has a finite number of possible outcomes
- A continuous distribution has an infinite number of possible outcomes

**Common Probability
Distributions**

CDF for a Continuous Distribution

The %ROE, x, for a firm is defined over
(−20, +30) and has a **CDF** of $F(x) = (x + 20) / 50$.
What is the probability that the ROE will be
positive and less than or equal to 15?

Prob $(0 \le x < 15) = F(15) - F(0)$

Prob $(x \le 15) = F(15) = (15 + 20) / 50 = 70\%$

Prob $(x \le 0) = F(0) = 20 / 50 = 40\%$

$70 - 40 = 30\%$

© Kaplan, Inc.

5-4

**Common Probability
Distributions**

Cumulative Distribution Function

A **cumulative distribution function (cdf)**, $F(x)$,
gives the probability that a random variable will be
less than or equal to a given value.

For the probability function:
$p(x) = x / 15$ for $X = \{1,2,3,4,5\}$

$F(3) = 1 / 15 + 2 / 15 + 3 / 15 = 6 / 15 = 40\%$

© Kaplan, Inc.

4

**Common Probability
Distributions**

Binomial Random Variable

The probability of exactly x <u>successes</u> in n
trials, given just two possible outcomes
(success and failure)

Probability of success on each trial (p) is
constant, and trials are independent

$$p(x) = \left(\frac{n!}{(n-x)!x!} \right) p^x (1-p)^{n-x}$$

$= nCx \; p^x (1-p)^{n-x}$

© Kaplan, Inc.

6

**Common Probability
Distributions**

Discrete Uniform

A <u>**discrete uniform distribution**</u> has a finite
number of possible outcomes, all of which are
equally likely

For example, $p(x) = 0.2$ for $X = \{1,2,3,4,5\}$

$p(2) = 20\%$

$F(3) = 60\%$

$Prob(2 \le X \le 4) = 60\%$

© Kaplan, Inc.

Slide 8-3 (upper left)

What is the probability of drawing exactly two white marbles from a bowl of white and black marbles in six tries if the probability of selecting white is 0.4 each time?

$x = 2, p = 0.4, n = 6$

$$p(x) = (nCx)p^x(1-p)^{n-x} = \left(\frac{n!}{(n-x)!x!}\right)p^x(1-p)^{n-x}$$

$$p(2) = 15(0.4)^2(1-0.4)^{6-2} = 0.31$$

© Kaplan, Inc.

8 - 3

Slide 9 (upper right)

Binomial Tree

Two possible outcomes each period, up or down

Prob (up move) + Prob (down move) = 1
Up factor (U) > 1   Down factor (D) = 1/U

Example:
Beginning stock price (S_0) = \$20
Prob up = 60% Prob down = 40%
Up factor = 1.12   Down factor 1 / 1.12

© Kaplan, Inc.

9

Slide 10 (lower left)

A Binomial Tree for Stock Price

P(up) = 60%   U = 1.12

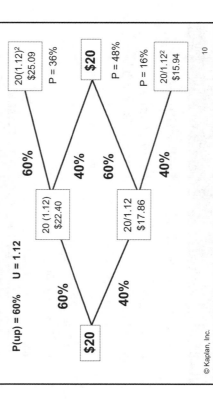

$20(1.12)^2$
\$25.09
P = 36%

20 (1.12)
\$22.40

\$20
P = 48%

\$20

20/1.12
\$17.86

$20/1.12^2$
\$15.94
P = 16%

60% 60% 60%
40% 40% 40%

© Kaplan, Inc.

10

Slide 11-2 (lower right)

A random variable follows a continuous uniform distribution over the interval 2 to 10. What is the probability of:

1. A value greater than 10.

2. A value between 3 and 5.

© Kaplan, Inc.

11 - 2

Common Probability
Distributions

Properties of Normal Distribution

- Completely described by **mean and variance**
- **Symmetric** about the mean (skewness = 0)
- **Kurtosis** (a measure of peakedness) = 3
- Linear combination of normally distributed random variables is also normally distributed
- Probabilities decrease further from the mean, but **the tails go on forever**

Multivariate normal: More than one random variable, need means, variances, and correlation coefficients

© Kaplan, Inc.

12

Common Probability
Distributions

Confidence Interval: Normal Distribution

Confidence interval: A range of values around an expected outcome. A random variable is expected to be in this range a certain percentage of the time.

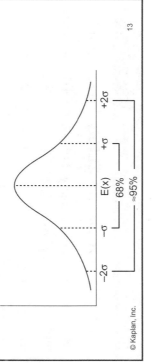

© Kaplan, Inc.

13

Common Probability
Distributions

Confidence Intervals: Normal Distribution

68% confidence interval = $\overline{X} \pm 1.00s$

90% confidence interval = $\overline{X} \pm 1.65s$

95% confidence interval = $\overline{X} \pm 1.96s$

99% confidence interval = $\overline{X} \pm 2.58s$

© Kaplan, Inc.

14

Common Probability
Distributions

The mean annual return (normally distributed) on a portfolio over many years is 11%, with a standard deviation of 8%. Calculate a 95% confidence interval on next year's return.

© Kaplan, Inc.

15 - 1

LOS 9.m Define/Explain/Calculate/Interpret
CFAI p. 534, Schweser p. 264

Common Probability
Distributions

Standard Normal Distribution

■ A normal distribution that has been standardized so that **mean = 0 and standard deviation = 1**

■ To standardize a random variable, calculate the z-value

■ Subtract the mean (so mean = 0) and divide by standard deviation (so σ = 1)

$$z = \frac{X - \mu}{\sigma}$$

> Z is the number of standard deviations from the mean

© Kaplan, Inc.

16

LOS 9.m Define/Explain/Calculate/Interpret
CFAI p. 534, Schweser p. 264

Common Probability
Distributions

The EPS for a large group of firms are normally distributed and have **μ = $4.00** and **σ = $1.50**. Find the probability that a randomly selected firm's earnings are less than $3.70.

$$z = \frac{3.70 - 4.00}{1.50} = -0.20$$

Z<0	.00	0.01
0.0	0.5000	0.4960
0.1	0.4602	0.4562
0.2	0.4207	0.4168

© Kaplan, Inc.

17 – 3

LOS 9.m Define/Explain/Calculate/Interpret
CFAI p. 534, Schweser p. 264

Common Probability
Distributions

Standard Normal Probabilities

There is a 42.07% probability that the EPS of a randomly selected firm will be more than 0.20 standard deviations below the mean (i.e., less than $3.70).

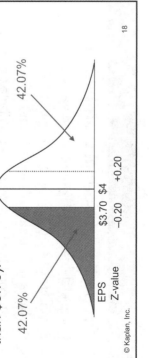

	42.07%
EPS	$3.70 $4
Z-value	−0.20 +0.20

© Kaplan, Inc.

18

LOS 9.n Define/Calculate/Select
CFAI p. 537, Schweser p. 267

Common Probability
Distributions

Shortfall Risk and Safety-First Ratio

Shortfall risk: Probability that a portfolio return or value will be below a target return or value

Roy's Safety-First Ratio: Number of std. dev. target is below the expected return/value

$$\text{SF Ratio} = \frac{\left[E(R_P) - R_L \right]}{\sigma_P}, \text{ where } R_L = \text{threshold/target return}$$

If R_L = Risk-free rate, SF Ratio is the same as Sharpe ratio

© Kaplan, Inc.

19

LOS 9.o Explain
CFAI p. 539, Schweser p. 269

Common Probability
Distributions

Lognormal Distribution

- If x is normal, e^x is lognormal

- Lognormal is always positive, used for modeling price relatives→ (1 + return) = e^x

Normal Distribution

Lognormal Distribution

© Kaplan, Inc.

21

LOS 9.p Distinguish/Calculate/Interpret
CFAI p. 541, Schweser p. 270

Common Probability
Distributions

Continuous Compounding

Continuously compounded rate = ln(1 + HPR)

EAY with continuous compounding = e^i − 1

1. If the 1-year HPR is 8%, what is the continuously compounded rate of return?

ln (1.08) = 7.7%

2. If the stated rate is 7.7%, with continuous compounding, what is the EAY?

EAY= $e^{0.077}$ − 1 = 8%

© Kaplan, Inc.

22 - 2

LOS 9.n Define/Calculate/Select
CFAI p. 537, Schweser p. 267

Common Probability
Distributions

Shortfall Risk and Safety-First Ratio

1. Given the two portfolios, which has the lower probability of generating a return below 5%?

Portfolio A has the larger SF ratio

$$\frac{(15 - 5)}{12} = 0.83$$

	Port. A	Port. B
E(R_P)	15%	18%
σ_P	12%	25%
SF Ratio	0.83	0.52
N(−SF Ratio)	0.2033	0.3015

2. Which portfolio has a lower shortfall risk?

Portfolio A has a 20.33% probability of a shortfall

© Kaplan, Inc.

20 - 3

Common Probability
Distributions

1. If the continuously compounded stated rate = 8%, what is the effective holding period return for one and one-half years?

2. How much will $1,200 grow to in one and one-half years?

© Kaplan, Inc.

23 - 2

LOS 9.q Explain/Describe
CFAI p. 545, Schweser p. 272

Common Probability
Distributions

Monte Carlo Simulation

Simulation can be used to estimate a distribution of derivatives prices or of NPVs

1. Specify distributions of random variables such as interest rates, underlying stock prices

2. Use computer random generation of variables

3. Value the derivative using those values

4. Repeat steps 2 and 3 1,000s of times

5. Calculate mean/variance of all values

© Kaplan, Inc.

24

LOS 9.r Compare
CFAI p. 550, Schweser p. 273

Common Probability
Distributions

Historical Simulation

Similar to Monte Carlo simulation, but generates random variables from distributions of **historical data**

Advantage: Don't have to estimate distribution of risk factors

Disadvantage: Future outcomes for risk factors may be outside the historical range

© Kaplan, Inc.

25

Common Probability
Distributions

Additional Learning Outcomes

LOS 9.h: calculate and interpret tracking error

© Kaplan, Inc.

26

Quantitative Methods

Quantitative Methods: Application

10. Sampling and Estimation

KAPLAN UNIVERSITY SCHOOL OF PROFESSIONAL AND CONTINUING EDUCATION | SCHWESER

LOS 10.c Distinguish
CFAI p. 567, Schweser p. 288   **Sampling and Estimation**

Stratified Random Sampling

1. **Create subgroups** from population based on important characteristics (e.g., identify bonds according to callable, ratings, maturity, coupon)

2. **Select samples** from each subgroup in proportion to the size of the subgroup

Used to:

- Construct a sample that matches the underlying population in certain characteristics
- Construct bond portfolios to track a bond index

© Kaplan, Inc.   29

LOS 10.f Calculate/Interpret
CFAI p. 572, Schweser p. 290   **Sampling and Estimation**

Standard Error of the Sample Mean

Standard error of sample mean is the standard deviation of the distribution of sample means for samples of size *n*.

$$\sigma_{\bar{x}} = \frac{\sigma}{\sqrt{n}} \text{ or } s_{\bar{x}} = \frac{s}{\sqrt{n}}$$

© Kaplan, Inc.   31

LOS 10.a,b Define/Explain
CFAI p. 566, Schweser p. 287   **Sampling and Estimation**

Sampling

- To make inferences about the parameters of a population, we will use a **sample**

- A **simple random sample** is one where every population member has an equal chance of being selected

- A sampling distribution is the distribution of sample statistics for repeated samples of size *n*

- **Sampling error** is the difference between a sample statistic and true population parameter (e.g., $\bar{x} - \mu$)

© Kaplan, Inc.   28

LOS 10.e Explain
CFAI p. 572, Schweser p. 289   **Sampling and Estimation**

Central Limit Theorem

For any population with mean *μ* and variance σ^2, as the size of a random sample gets large, the distribution of sample means approaches a normal distribution with **mean *μ* and variance σ^2/n**

Allows us to make inferences about and construct **confidence intervals** for population means based on sample means

© Kaplan, Inc.   30

Sampling and Estimation

LOS 10.g Identify/Describe
CFAI p. 576, Schweser p. 292

Desirable Estimator Properties

1. **Unbiased** – expected value equal to parameter

2. **Efficient** – sampling distribution has smallest variance of all unbiased estimators

3. **Consistent** – larger sample → better estimator

   Standard error of estimate decreases with larger sample size

© Kaplan, Inc.

33

Sampling and Estimation

LOS 10.i Describe/Calculate/Interpret
CFAI p. 580, Schweser p. 292

Student's *t*-Distribution and Degrees of Freedom

Properties of Student's *t*-Distribution

- Symmetrical (bell shaped)
- Fatter tails than a normal distribution
- Defined by single parameter, degrees of freedom (df), where df = n − 1
- As df increase, *t*-distribution <u>approaches</u> <u>normal distribution</u>

© Kaplan, Inc.

35

Sampling and Estimation

The mean P/E for a sample of 41 firms is 19.0 and the standard deviation of the population is 6.6. What is the standard error of the sample mean?

$$\sigma_{\bar{x}} = \frac{\sigma}{\sqrt{n}} = \frac{6.6}{\sqrt{41}} = 1.03$$

For samples of size n = 41, the distribution of the **sample means** has a mean of 19.0 and a standard deviation of 1.03.

© Kaplan, Inc.

32 - 2

Sampling and Estimation

LOS 10.h Distinguish
CFAI p. 577, Schweser p. 292

The mean P/E for a sample of 41 firms is 19.0. The std dev of the sample is 6.6, and the population is approximately normal. Calculate:

1. A 90% confidence interval for the mean

2. 95% confidence interval

3. 95% confidence interval for P/E of a random firm

© Kaplan, Inc.

34 - 3

Slide 37

Confidence Intervals for Mean

When sampling from a:		Reliability Factors	
Distribution	Variance	Small Sample (n < 30)	Large Sample (n > 30)
Normal	Known	z-statistic	z-statistic
Normal	Unknown	t-statistic	t-statistic*
Nonnormal	Known	Not available	z-statistic
Nonnormal	Unknown	Not available	t-statistic*

*The z-statistic is theoretically acceptable

© Kaplan, Inc.

37

Slide 39

Sample Size Issues

We've seen that larger samples produce better estimates and smaller confidence intervals, **but:**

Cost can be a factor—obtaining more data can increase costs, so there is a trade-off

Including more data points from a population (time period) with *different parameters* will not improve your estimate

© Kaplan, Inc.

39

Slide 36

t-Distribution

The figure below shows the shape of the t-distribution with different degrees of freedom.

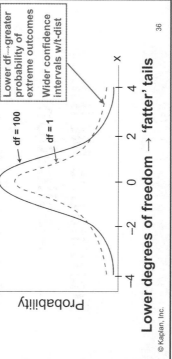

Lower df → greater probability of extreme outcomes

Wider confidence intervals w/t-dist

df = 100

df = 1

Lower degrees of freedom → 'fatter' tails

© Kaplan, Inc.

36

Slide 38-3

Confidence Interval for Mean

The sample mean is 19.0, the sample standard deviation is 6.6, and n = 41. Establish a 90% confidence interval for the population mean.

standard error of mean $= \dfrac{s}{\sqrt{n}} = \dfrac{6.6}{\sqrt{41}} = 1.03$

From t-table, reliability factor is 1.684 (df = 40, a/2 = 0.05)

degrees of freedom   5% in each tail

$19.0 \pm 1.684\,(1.03) = 17.27 < \text{mean} < 20.73$

© Kaplan, Inc.

38 - 3

Types of Bias

Data-mining bias – from repeatedly doing tests on same data sample

Sample selection bias – sample not really random

Survivorship bias – sampling only surviving firms, mutual funds, hedge funds

Look-ahead bias – using information not available at the time to construct sample

Time-period bias – relationship exists only during the time period of sample data

© Kaplan, Inc.

40

Additional Learning Outcomes

LOS 10.d: time series, cross-sectional data

© Kaplan, Inc.

41

Quantitative Methods: Application

11. Hypothesis Testing

Steps in Hypothesis Testing

- State the hypothesis—relation to be tested
- Select a test statistic
- Specify the level of significance
- State the decision rule for the hypothesis
- Collect the sample and calculate statistics
- Make a decision about the hypothesis
- Make a decision based on the test results

© Kaplan, Inc.

43

LOS 11.a Define/Describe/Interpret
CFAI p. 607, Schweser p. 310   **Hypothesis Testing**

Null and Alternative Hypotheses

Null hypothesis (H_0)
1. The hypothesis to be tested
2. Researcher wants to reject it
3. Always includes the equal sign

Alternative hypothesis (H_a)
1. What the researcher would like to conclude
2. Supported if the researcher rejects the null hypothesis

© Kaplan, Inc.   44

LOS 11.c Explain
CFAI p. 609, Schweser p. 315   **Hypothesis Testing**

Test Statistic and Critical Values

- A test statistic is (1) calculated from sample data and (2) compared to critical value(s) to test H_0

- If the test statistic exceeds the critical value (or is outside the range of critical values), the researcher rejects H_0

- Critical values are like a confidence interval

© Kaplan, Inc.   45

LOS 11.b Distinguish
CFAI p. 608, Schweser p. 311   **Hypothesis Testing**

Two-Tailed Test

Use when testing to see if a population parameter is different from a specified value

$$H_0: \mu = 0 \text{ versus } H_a: \mu \neq 0$$

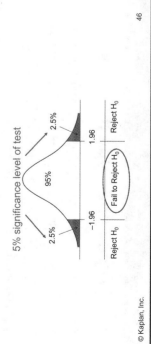

© Kaplan, Inc.   46

LOS 11.b Distinguish
CFAI p. 608, Schweser p. 311   **Hypothesis Testing**

One-Tailed Test

Use when testing to see if a parameter is <u>above</u> or <u>below</u> a specified value

$$H_0: \mu \leq 0 \text{ versus } H_a: \mu > 0$$
$$H_0: \mu \geq 0 \text{ versus } H_a: \mu < 0$$

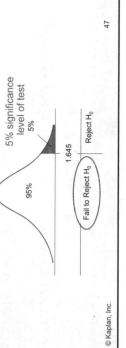
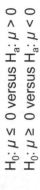

© Kaplan, Inc.   47

46

LOS 11.c,d Explain
CFAI p. 609, Schweser p. 315
Hypothesis Testing

Type I and Type II Errors

Type I Error: Rejecting H_0 when it is actually true

Type II Error: Failing to reject H_0 when it is false

Significance level is Probability of Type I Error
[e.g., convicting an innocent person (null is innocent)]

Power of test is 1 − Prob. of Type II Error
(e.g., failing to convict a guilty person)

© Kaplan, Inc.

48

LOS 11.e Distinguish
CFAI p. 615, Schweser p. 319
Hypothesis Testing

Statistically vs.
Economically Meaningful Result

Statistical significance does not necessarily imply **economic significance:**

- Transactions costs
- Taxes
- Risk

© Kaplan, Inc.

49

LOS 11.f Explain/Interpret
CFAI p. 615, Schweser p. 320
Hypothesis Testing

p-value Example

A *p*-value is the smallest level of significance at which the null can be rejected, the probability of getting the test statistic by chance if the null is true.

If the *p*-value is given as 0.0213 or 2.13%:

We **can** reject the null at 5% significance.

We **can** reject the null at 3% significance.

We **cannot** reject the null at 1% significance.

© Kaplan, Inc.

50

Hypothesis Testing

Data for a fund:

Sample mean = 1.5%   Sample size = 45
Population std dev = 1.4%   Population non-normal

Can we reject the hypothesis that a fund's mean return is equal to 1% per month, at the 95% level?

© Kaplan, Inc.

51 - 3

LOS 11.g Identify/Interpret
CFAI p. 616, Schweser p. 321 — **Hypothesis Testing**

Hypothesis Testing

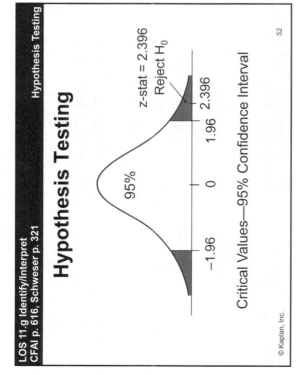

Critical Values—95% Confidence Interval

© Kaplan, Inc.   52

LOS 11.h,i Identify/Interpret
CFAI p. 623, Schweser p. 324 — **Hypothesis Testing**

Test Statistics

LOS: **Identify** the appropriate test statistic and interpret the results...

Difference in means test: Use sample means from two independent normal populations, *t*-test, reject if test statistic is outside critical values.

Mean differences (paired comparison) test: Use sample of paired observations from two dependent normal populations, *t*-test, reject if test statistic is outside critical values.

© Kaplan, Inc.   53

LOS 11.j Identify/Interpret
CFAI p. 632, Schweser p. 332 — **Hypothesis Testing**

Other Tests

Test of whether the variance of a normal population equals σ_0^2 uses a **Chi-square** test statistic, two-tailed test, reject if outside the critical values

Test of whether the variances of two normal populations are equal is an **F-test**

Putting the larger sample variance in the numerator allows us to **consider only upper critical value** — although F-test is a two-tailed test

© Kaplan, Inc.   54

LOS 11.k Distinguish/Describe
CFAI p. 637, Schweser p. 339 — **Hypothesis Testing**

Parametric and Nonparametric Tests

- **Parametric tests** are based on assumptions about population distributions and population parameters (e.g., *t*-test, *z*-test, F-test)

- **Nonparametric tests** make few if any assumptions about the population distribution and test things other than parameter values (e.g., runs tests, rank correlation tests)

© Kaplan, Inc.   55

Quantitative Methods

Quantitative Methods: Application

12. Technical Analysis

KAPLAN UNIVERSITY | SCHOOL OF PROFESSIONAL AND CONTINUING EDUCATION | SCHWESER

LOS 12.a Explain
CFAI p. 660, Schweser p. 350

Technical Analysis

Principles and Assumptions of Technical Analysis

- Stock values determined by **supply and demand which are driven by both rational and irrational behavior**

- Technical analysts use prices and trading volume to analyze changes in supply and demand

- Security **prices move in trends** that persist for long periods and repeat themselves in predictable ways

© Kaplan, Inc.

57

LOS 12.a Explain
CFAI p. 660, Schweser p. 350

Technical Analysis

Technical Analysis vs. Fundamental Analysis

- **Fundamental analysts** look for changes in intrinsic values (what prices **should** be) based primarily on anticipated financial results and estimates of future cash flows

- **Technical analysts** try to predict price change though analysis of past trading prices and volume

© Kaplan, Inc.

58

LOS 12.a Explain
CFAI p. 660, Schweser p. 350

Technical Analysis

Claimed Advantages of Technical Analysis

- It is based on actual trade data, whereas fundamental analysis is based on accounting numbers which can be estimates

- Can be used for assets with **no cash flows** to be discounted for valuation (e.g., commodities)

- Don't have to learn accounting!
  LOS b, c, d, e, f, g, and h are left for self-study

© Kaplan, Inc.

59

Quantitative Methods

Additional Problems

KAPLAN UNIVERSITY | SCHOOL OF PROFESSIONAL AND CONTINUING EDUCATION | SCHWESER

© Kaplan, Inc.

Common Probability Distributions

Additional Study

LOS 12.b: technical analysis charts

LOS 12.c: trend, support, resistance

LOS 12.d: chart patterns

LOS 12.e: technical analysis indicators

LOS 12.f: cycles

LOS 12.g: Elliott wave theory

LOS 12.h: intermarket analysis

© Kaplan, Inc.

60

Additional Problems

2) Free cash flow per share for a population of companies is approximately normal, has a mean of $2.50, and a standard deviation of $0.50. The probability that a firm chosen at random will have cash flow per share of less than $2.00 is:

A. 16%.

B. 50%.

C. 84%.

© Kaplan, Inc.

- 1

Additional Problems

1) Returns on an index of 100 stocks are approximately normal, have a mean of 9% and std. dev. of 15%. A 99% confidence interval on next year's index return is:

A. –20.4% to 38.4%.

B. –29.7% to 47.7%.

C. 5.1% to 12.9%.

© Kaplan, Inc.

- 3

Additional Problems

3) A sample of 64 high-yield bond returns was taken from a normally distributed population. The sample mean was 14%, and the sample standard deviation was 25%. The 95% confidence interval in which the population mean lies is *closest* to:

A. 13% to 15%.

B. 11% to 17%.

C. 8% to 20%.

© Kaplan, Inc.

- 4

Additional Problems

4) A sample of 9 high-yield bond returns was taken from a normally distributed population. The population has a mean of 16% and a variance of 144. If a bond from the population is randomly selected, a 90% confidence interval for its return is:

A. −3.74% to 35.74%.

B. 0.64% to 31.36%.

C. 11.26% to 16.74%.

© Kaplan, Inc.

- 4

Additional Problems
CFA Curriculum Vol. 1, R.11, Q.16, p. 649

5) All else equal, is specifying a smaller significance level in a hypothesis test likely to increase the probability of a:

	Type I error?	Type II error?
A.	No	No
B.	No	Yes
C.	Yes	Yes

- 3

Additional Questions
CFA Curriculum Vol. 1, R.11, Q.17, p. 650

6) All else equal, is increasing the sample size for a hypothesis test likely to decrease the probability of a:

	Type I error?	Type II error?
A.	No	No
B.	No	Yes
C.	Yes	Yes

- 3

Additional Problems

8. The probability that a stock's return will be greater than the return on an index in any given week is 60%. The probability that the stock's return will be greater than the return on the index in 31 weeks out of the 52 weeks next year is *closest* to:

A. 11%.

B. 13%.

C. 15%.

- 3

Additional Problems

7) Quarterly returns on an index are approximately normally distributed with a standard deviation of 10%. Index returns over the most recent 20 quarters have a mean of 4%. Should a researcher who wants to show that the average quarterly returns for this index are positive reject the null hypothesis at the 5% significance level?

- 3

Additional Problems

9. The continuously compounded rate of return on an investment is 4.4%. Its effective annual return is *closest* to:

A. 4.45%.

B. 4.50%.

C. 4.55%.

- 2

STUDY SESSION 3 ANSWERS

Reading	Slide Number	Answer
9	11(1)	0
9	11(2)	25%
9	15	−4.7% to 26.7%
9	23(1)	12.75%
9	23(2)	$1.353
10	34(1)	17.3 < mean < 20.7
10	34(2)	17.0 < mean < 21.0
10	34(3)	6.06 < P/E < 31.94
11	51	z-stat = 2.396; reject

Additional Problems

1. B

2. A

3. C

4. A

5. B

6. C

7. z-stat = 1.789; reject

8. A

9. B

Study Session 4

Economics: Microeconomic Analysis

Economics

Economics: Microeconomic Analysis

13. Demand and Supply Analysis: Introduction

KAPLAN UNIVERSITY | SCHOOL OF PROFESSIONAL AND CONTINUING EDUCATION | SCHWESER

Economics

Study Session 4
Economics: Microeconomic Analysis

13. Demand and Supply Analysis: Introduction
14. Demand and Supply Analysis: Consumer Demand
15. Demand and Supply Analysis: The Firm
16. The Firm and Market Structures

KAPLAN UNIVERSITY | SCHOOL OF PROFESSIONAL AND CONTINUING EDUCATION | SCHWESER

LOS 13.c Describe
CFAI p. 11 Schweser p. 12

Demand and Supply
Analysis: Introduction

Change in Quantity Demanded

Changes in own price (P_x) cause movements along the supply and demand curves.

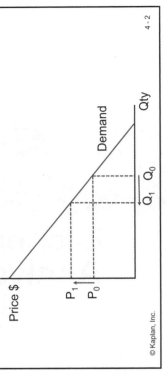

© Kaplan, Inc.

4 - 2

LOS 13.b Explain
CFAI p. 8 Schweser p. 10

Demand and Supply
Analysis: Introduction

Principles of Supply and Demand

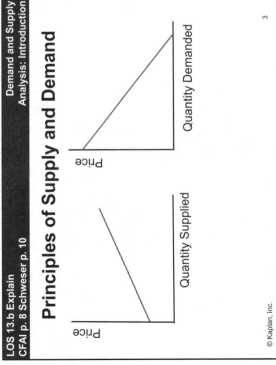

© Kaplan, Inc.

3

Change in Demand

Changes in *other factors of demand* will shift the curve:

- Income levels
- Price of substitutes
- Price of complements

Changes in *other factors of supply* will shift the curve:

- Raw materials price
- Labor costs
- Overheads
- Technology

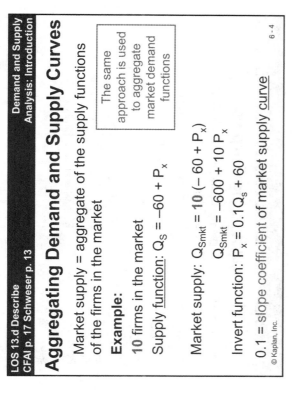

Decrease in demand   Increase in demand

Price

Quantity

Decrease in supply   Increase in supply

Price

Quantity

© Kaplan, Inc.

5 - 4

Aggregating Demand and Supply Curves

Market supply = aggregate of the supply functions of the firms in the market

> The same approach is used to aggregate market demand functions

Example:

10 firms in the market

Supply function: $Q_S = -60 + P_x$

Market supply: $Q_{Smkt} = 10 (-60 + P_x)$

$Q_{Smkt} = -600 + 10 P_x$

Invert function: $P_x = 0.1 Q_s + 60$

0.1 = slope coefficient of market supply curve

© Kaplan, Inc.

6 - 4

Movement to Equilibrium

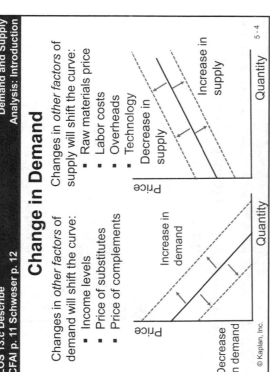

Price £

£50

P equilibrium

Supply > Demand
Excess Supply

Supply (MC)

Suppliers decrease price

Consumers bid up price

Demand > Supply
Excess Demand

Demand (MB)

Q equilibrium   Quantity

© Kaplan, Inc.

7 - 3

Calculation of Equilibrium Price

Supply: $Q_S = -600 + 10 P_x$

Demand: $Q_D = 3,000 - 15 P_x$

At Equilibrium: $-600 + 10 P_x = 3,000 - 15 P_x$

Solve for P_x: $3,600 = 25 P_x$ $P_x = 144$ $Q_E = 840$

This is partial equilibrium analysis, only the effects of own price changes are considered

General equilibrium considers the effects of a change in own price on prices of other goods etc.

© Kaplan, Inc.

8 - 3

Slide 10-5 — Consumer Surplus

Demand and Supply
Analysis: Introduction

Consumer Surplus

Difference between price paid and marginal benefit

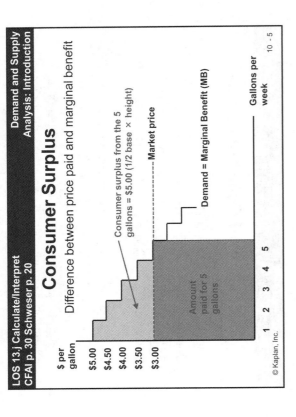

Consumer surplus from the 5 gallons = $5.00 (1/2 base × height)

Market price

Amount paid for 5 gallons

Demand = Marginal Benefit (MB)

$ per gallon: $5.00, $4.50, $4.00, $3.50, $3.00

Gallons per week: 1 2 3 4 5

© Kaplan, Inc.

10 - 5

Slide 12-5 — Calculating Surplus

Demand and Supply
Analysis: Introduction

Calculating Surplus

Demand Function = $Q_D = 3,000 - 15P_x$
Supply Function = $Q_S = -600 + 10P_x$

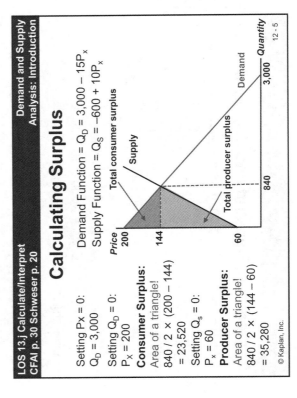

Total consumer surplus

Supply

Total producer surplus

Demand

Price: 200, 144, 60

Quantity: 840, 3,000

Setting Px = 0:
$Q_D = 3,000$
Setting $Q_D = 0$:
$P_x = 200$
Consumer Surplus:
Area of a triangle!
$840 / 2 \times (200 - 144)$
$= 23,520$
Setting $Q_S = 0$:
$P_x = 60$
Producer Surplus:
Area of a triangle!
$840 / 2 \times (144 - 60)$
$= 35,280$

© Kaplan, Inc.

12 - 5

Slide 9-4 — Excess Demand or Supply

Demand and Supply
Analysis: Introduction

Excess Demand or Supply

Supply function: $Q_S = -600 + 10P_x$
Demand function: $Q_D = 3,000 - 15P_x$

At a price of 120:   Price < Equilibrium

$Q_S = -600 + (10 \times 120) = 600$
$Q_D = 3,000 - (15 \times 120) = 1,200$ } Excess demand = 600

At a price of 160:   Price > Equilibrium

$Q_S = -600 + (10 \times 160) = 1,000$
$Q_D = 3,000 - (15 \times 160) = 600$ } Excess supply = 400

© Kaplan, Inc.

9 - 4

Slide 11-1 — Marginal (Opportunity) Cost and Producer Surplus

Demand and Supply
Analysis: Introduction

Marginal (Opportunity) Cost and Producer Surplus

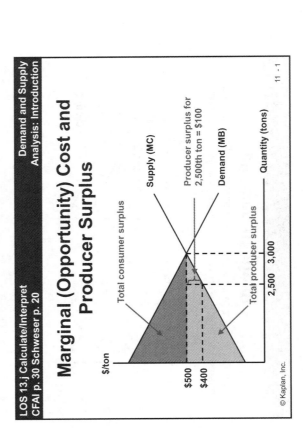

$/ton

Total consumer surplus

Supply (MC)

Producer surplus for 2,500th ton = $100

Demand (MB)

Total producer surplus

$500, $400

Quantity (tons): 2,500 3,000

© Kaplan, Inc.

11 - 1

**CFA Curriculum Vol. 2,
R.13, Q.20, p. 58**

Assume a market demand function is given by the equation $Q^d = 50 - 0.75P$ where Q^d is the quantity demanded and P is the price. If $P = 10$ the consumer surplus is *closest* to:

A. 67.

B. 1,205.

C. 16.67.

13 - 3

LOS 13.k Describe
CFAI p. 36, Schweser p. 24

Price Ceiling Decreases P_E and Q_E

14 - 2

LOS 13.k Describe
CFAI p. 36, Schweser p. 24

Price Floors Increase P_E, Decrease Q_E

15 - 3

**CFA Curriculum Vol. 2,
R.13, Q.17, p. 58**

Which of the following statements *most* accurately and completely describes a deadweight loss?

A. A transfer of surplus from one party to another.

B. A reduction in either the buyer's or seller's surplus.

C. A reduction in total surplus resulting from market interference.

16 - 1

LOS 13.k Describe
CFAI p. 36, Schweser p. 24

**Demand and Supply
Analysis: Introduction**

Effect of Taxes

For a tax paid paid by sellers:

- Price paid by buyers (including tax) increases
- Price received by sellers (without tax) decreases
- Quantity bought and sold decreases
- Same effects for per unit tax on buyers

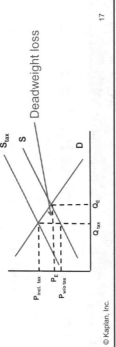

© Kaplan, Inc.

17

CFA Curriculum Vol. 2,
R.13, Q.19, p. 58

A quota on an imported good below the market-clearing quantity will most likely lead to which of the following effects?

A. The supply curve shifts upward.

B. The demand curve shifts upward.

C. Some of the buyer's surplus transfers to the seller.

18 - 1

LOS 13.m Calculate/Interpret/Describe
CFAI p. 43 Schweser p. 32

**Demand and Supply
Analysis: Introduction**

Price Elasticity of Demand

Price Elasticity of Demand (PED) = $\dfrac{\%\Delta Q}{\%\Delta P_X}$

As the price of a normal good increases, **quantity demanded** decreases

- **Elastic demand**: Percentage increase in price leads to a larger percentage decrease in quantity demanded
- **Inelastic demand**: Percentage increase in price leads to a smaller percentage decrease in quantity demanded

© Kaplan, Inc.

19

LOS 13.m Calculate/Interpret/Describe
CFAI p. 43 Schweser p. 32

**Demand and Supply
Analysis: Introduction**

Factors That Influence Elasticity of Demand

- Availability and closeness of **substitutes**

   ↑ Substitutes: ↑ Elasticity

- **Proportion of income** spent on the item

   ↑ Proportion of income: ↑ Elasticity

- **Time** elapsed since previous price change

   ↑ Time: ↑ Elasticity

© Kaplan, Inc.

20 - 3

Price Elasticity of Demand

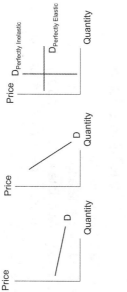

Elastic

Price

D

Quantity

Inelastic

Price

D

Quantity

Perfectly Inelastic/Elastic

Price $D_{Perfectly\ Inelastic}$

$D_{Perfectly\ Elastic}$

Quantity

© Kaplan, Inc.

21

Elasticity on a Straight-line Demand Curve

> Slope of demand curve ≠ price elasticity
>
> Slope depends on units price and quantity are measured in. Elasticity is based on % change

Price($)

8
7
6
5
4
3
2
1

(a) high elasticity

(b) unitary elasticity
    elasticity = −1

(c) low elasticity

10 20 30 40 50 60 70 80   Quantity

© Kaplan, Inc.

22

Calculating Elasticity at a Point

Price elasticity of demand (PED) = $\dfrac{\%\Delta Q}{\%\Delta P_X}$

$$\frac{\%\Delta Q}{\%\Delta P_X} = \frac{\Delta Q/Q_0}{\Delta P_X/P_0} = \frac{P_0}{Q_0}\times\boxed{\frac{\Delta Q}{\Delta P_X}}$$

→ Slope coefficient of price (−140)

Calculate PED at a price of €150:

$Q_{DX} = 29,500 - 140\,P_X$

$Q_{DX} = 29,500 - (140 \times 150)$

$Q_{DX} = 8,500$

$$PED = \left(\frac{150}{8,500}\right)\times(-140) = -2.47$$

© Kaplan, Inc.

23 - 2

Arc Elasticity of Demand

The price of gasoline increases from $4/gallon to $5/gallon, reducing the quantity demanded from 11,000 to 9,000 gallons. Calculate the price (arc) elasticity of demand.

$$\frac{\%\,change\ in\ price}{\%\,change\ in\ quantity} = \frac{\dfrac{5-4}{\boxed{\dfrac{5+4}{2}}}}{\dfrac{9,000-11,000}{\boxed{\dfrac{9,000+11,000}{2}}}} = \frac{22.2\%}{-20.0\%} = -1.11$$

© Kaplan, Inc.

24

60

Slide (top left):

Cross Price Elasticity of Demand

Price of coffee increased 16.65% and demand for tea increased 11.10%.

$$\text{cross price elasticity of demand} = \frac{11.10\%}{16.65\%} = 0.67$$

cross price elasticity > 0: the goods are *substitutes*

Price of pizza increased 25.0% and demand for cola decreased 10.7%.

$$\text{cross price elasticity of demand} = \frac{-10.7\%}{25.0\%} = -0.43$$

cross price elasticity < 0: the goods are *complements*

© Kaplan, Inc.

Slide (top right):

Economics:
Microeconomic Analysis

14. Demand and Supply Analysis: Consumer Demand

KAPLAN UNIVERSITY SCHOOL OF PROFESSIONAL AND CONTINUING EDUCATION | SCHWESER

Slide (bottom left):

Income Elasticity of Demand

The sensitivity of quantity demanded to changes in income

$$\text{income elasticity} = \frac{\%\text{ change in quantity demanded}}{\%\text{ change in income}}$$

Normal good: Income↑ Demand↑ Elasticity > 0

Inferior good: Income↑ Demand↓ Elasticity < 0 (e.g., bus travel)

25

© Kaplan, Inc.

Slide (bottom right):

Additional LOS

LOS 13.a: types of markets

LOS 13.f: stable and unstable equilibria

LOS 13.g: calculate demand and supply functions, interpret demand and supply curves

LOS 13.i: auctions

LOS 13.l: effects on price/quantity of removing floor, ceiling, subsidy, tax, quota

27

© Kaplan, Inc.

Utility Theory

Non-satiation: More is always preferred to less

Completeness: All combinations of goods can be ranked by preferences

Transitivity: If A is preferred to B and B is preferred to C, A must be preferred to C

Utility function: Utility = $U(Q_1, Q_2, Q_3, \ldots, Q_N)$

- Variables are quantity consumed of goods 1 to N
- Quantity must be ≥ 0 for each good
- Utility is an ordinal scale

© Kaplan, Inc.   29

An Indifference Curve

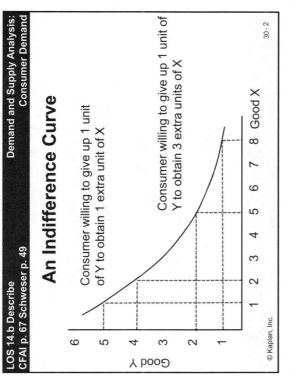

Consumer willing to give up 1 unit of Y to obtain 1 extra unit of X

Consumer willing to give up 1 unit of Y to obtain 3 extra units of X

© Kaplan, Inc.   30-2

Budget Constraint

- Based on consumer's income and the prices of the products
- Budget line shows all combinations of both goods that will exhaust the consumer's income

Income = $4,000
$P_X = \$80$
$P_Y = \$200$

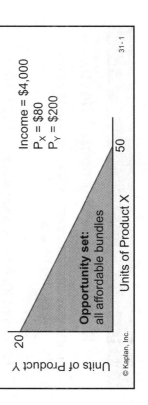

Opportunity set:
all affordable bundles

Units of Product X

© Kaplan, Inc.   31-1

Consumer's Equilibrium Bundle

Income = $4,000
$P_X = \$80$
$P_Y = \$200$

I_0: Suboptimal; full income not consumed, utility not maximized

I_2: Utility > I_1 but not affordable

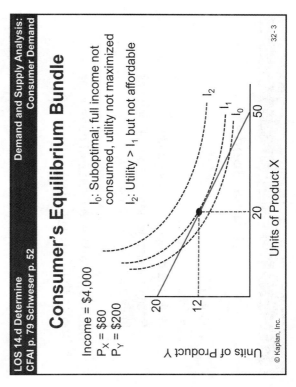

Units of Product X

© Kaplan, Inc.   32-3

62

LOS 14.f Distinguish/Explain
CFAI p. 87 Schweser p. 55

Veblen Good

- Higher price increases desirability
  - ↑ Price: ↑ status
- High end designer/luxury goods
- Positively sloped demand curve for some individuals (within a range)

Not supported by the rules of consumer choice (but Giffen good is)

© Kaplan, Inc.

34

Economics: Microeconomic Analysis

15. Demand and Supply Analysis: The Firm

LOS 14.e,f Compare/Distinguish/Explain
CFAI p. 84 Schweser p. 52

Substitution and Income Effects

Substitution effect *always* shifts consumption to more of Good X when the price of Good X falls

Total expenditure on the original bundle is now less than full income (budget line shifts)

- Normal goods: Increase in income increases consumption of Good X
  - Inferior goods: Increase in income decreases consumption of Good X

Giffen good: Negative income effect > positive substitution effect of price decrease, Q_D falls

© Kaplan, Inc.

33

CFA Curriculum Vol. 2,
R.14, Q.6, p. 92

In the case of a normal good with a decrease in own price, which of the following statements is *most likely* true?

A. Both the substitution and income effects lead to an increase in the quantity purchased.

B. The substitution effect leads to an increase in the quantity purchased, while the income effect has no impact.

C. The substitution effect leads to an increase in the quantity purchased, while the income effect leads to a decrease.

35 - 1

LOS 15.a Calculate/Interpret/Compare
CFAI p. 97 Schweser p. 60
Demand and Supply
Analysis: The Firm

Economic Profit

Accounting profit = revenue – explicit costs

Economic profit = accounting profit – implicit costs

Implicit costs = return on owner capital
+ opportunity cost of owner's time

Normal profit when economic profit = 0

Economic rent = surplus value when resource is in fixed supply, price > amount required to sustain supply

© Kaplan, Inc.   37

LOS 15.b Calculate/Interpret/Compare
CFAI p. 101 Schweser p. 64
Demand and Supply
Analysis: The Firm

Price, Marginal Revenue, Average Revenue

Total Revenue = P X Q
Average Revenue = TR/Q = Price
Marginal Revenue = ΔTR/ΔQ

P_M = Market Price = MR = AR

Price

P_M ——————————— Demand

Quantity

© Kaplan, Inc.   38

LOS 15.b Calculate/Interpret/Compare
CFAI p. 101 Schweser p. 64
Demand and Supply
Analysis: The Firm

Price, Marginal Revenue, and Average Revenue

Sell 3 @ 60: TR = 180
Sell 4 @ 50: TR = 200
MR for 4th Unit = 20
AR = Price

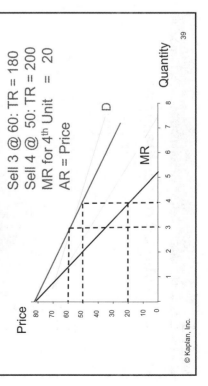

© Kaplan, Inc.   39

LOS 15.c Describe
CFAI p. 108 Schweser p. 66
Demand and Supply
Analysis: The Firm

Factors of Production

Land – location

Labor – skilled, unskilled, management

Capital – equipment, tools, buildings

Materials – productive inputs

© Kaplan, Inc.   40

LOS 15.d Calculate/Interpret
CFAI p. 109 Schweser p. 68

Total Costs for the Firm

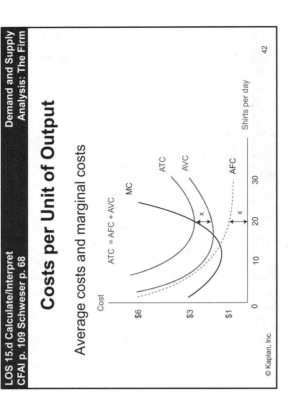

© Kaplan, Inc.

41

LOS 15.d Calculate/Interpret
CFAI p. 109 Schweser p. 68

Costs per Unit of Output

Average costs and marginal costs

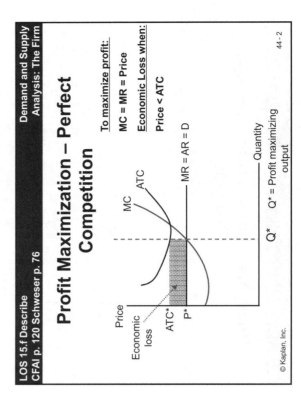

© Kaplan, Inc.

42

LOS 15.e Determine/Describe
CFAI p. 116 Schweser p. 72

Breakeven and Shutdown

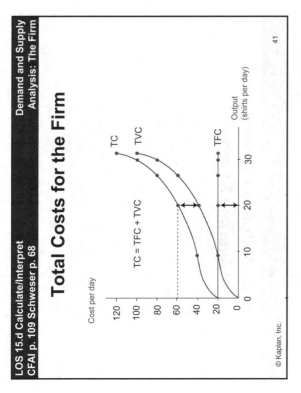

© Kaplan, Inc.

43 - 3

LOS 15.f Describe
CFAI p. 120 Schweser p. 76

Profit Maximization – Perfect Competition

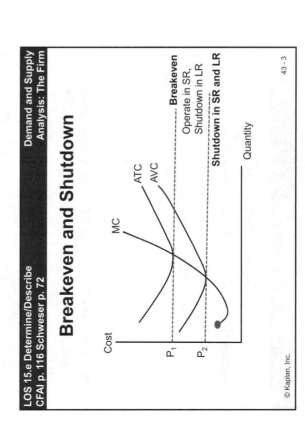

© Kaplan, Inc.

44 - 2

Profit Maximization – Imperfect Competition

Profit is maximized at the output for which:
marginal cost = marginal revenue

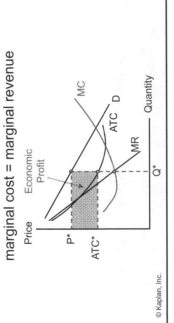

© Kaplan, Inc.

45 - 2

Profit Maximization in the Long Run

Under perfect competition, the market price will be P_2 in the long run as firms move to minimum efficient scale

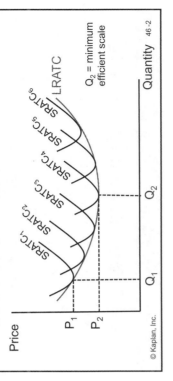

© Kaplan, Inc.

46 -2

A profit maximum is *least likely* to occur when:

A. average total cost is minimized.

B. marginal revenue equals marginal cost.

C. the difference between total revenue and total cost is maximized.

47 - 1

Long-Run Industry Costs

Increasing-cost industry: Resource costs increase with greater industry output, long-run industry supply is upward sloping (e.g., oil production)

Decreasing-cost industry: Resource costs decrease with greater industry output, long-run industry supply is downward sloping (e.g., flat screen televisions, semiconductors, PCs) (suppliers have economies of scale, production learning curve, etc.)

If resource prices are constant, then long-run supply is horizontal (i.e., **constant-cost industry**)

© Kaplan, Inc.

48

Total, Marginal, and Average Product of Labor

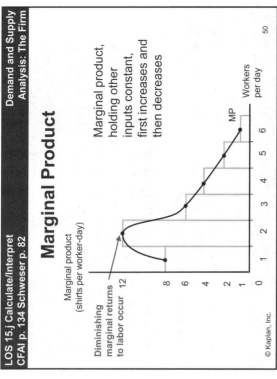

Workers	Total Product	Marginal Product	Average Product
1	8	8	8
2	20	12	10
3	26	6	8.7
4	30	4	7.5
5	32	2	6.4
6	33	1	5.5

33 ÷ 6 = 5.5

© Kaplan, Inc.   49

Marginal Product

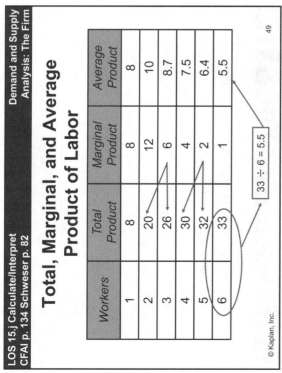

Marginal product
(shirts per worker-day)

Diminishing
marginal returns
to labor occur

Marginal product,
holding other
inputs constant,
first increases and
then decreases

MP

Workers
per day

© Kaplan, Inc.   50

Marginal and Average Product

AP & MP
(shirts per day per
worker)

Diminishing marginal returns
to labor occur

Maximum average product

AP

MP

Labor
(workers per day)

© Kaplan, Inc.   51

Profit Maximizing Input Amounts

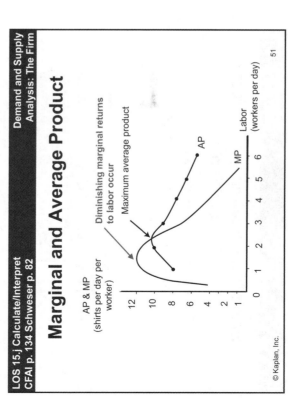

- Marginal revenue product (MRP) is the addition to total revenue from selling the additional output (MP) from employing one more unit of an input.

- As each extra unit of input is added, output increases but at a decreasing rate (diminishing marginal returns).

  - To maximize profits, use additional amounts of an input until **MRP = unit costs**.

  - Labor: Hire more workers until MRP_L = wage

© Kaplan, Inc.   52

Minimizing the Cost of Production

To minimize costs, it must be the case that:

$$\frac{MP_A}{P_A} = \frac{MP_B}{P_B} = \frac{MP_C}{P_C}$$

- The additional output per dollar spent on each input must be equal at the margin.

- If $MP_L/P_L > MP_K/P_K$, then using more labor and less capital to produce the output will decrease costs.

© Kaplan, Inc.

53

A firm employs unskilled and skilled labor in a cost-minimizing mix at its manufacturing plant. The marginal product of unskilled labor is less than that of skilled labor. Wages for unskilled labor are 300 pesos per day and 500 pesos per day for skilled labor. If a new law imposes a minimum wage of 400 pesos per day the firm will *most likely* employ:

A. more skilled workers.

B. more unskilled workers.

C. less skilled and less unskilled workers.

© Kaplan, Inc.

54 - 1

Economics

Economics: Microeconomic Analysis

16. The Firm and Market Structures

KAPLAN UNIVERSITY SCHOOL OF PROFESSIONAL AND CONTINUING EDUCATION | SCHWESER

Characteristics of Market Structures

	Perfect Competition	Monopolistic Competition	Oligopoly	Monopoly
Number of sellers	Many firms	Many firms	Few firms	Single firm
Barriers to entry	Very low	Low	High	Very high
Nature of substitute products	Very good substitutes	Good substitutes but differentiated	Very good substitutes or differentiated	No good substitutes
Nature of competition	Price only	Price, marketing, features	Price, marketing, features	Advertising
Price power	None	Some	Some to significant	Significant

© Kaplan, Inc.

56

68

LOS 16.b,d,e Explain/Describe/Determine
CFAI p. 156 Schweser p. 96

Perfect Competition

Firms in perfect competition are **price takers**

- No influence over market price
- "Take" the equilibrium (market) price as given

Characteristics:

- Homogeneous product
- Large number of independent firms; each small relative to the total market
- Perfectly elastic demand curves
- No barriers to entry or exit
- Supply and demand determine market price

© Kaplan, Inc.

57

LOS 16.b,d,e Explain/Describe/Determine
CFAI p. 156 Schweser p. 96

Perfect Competition
Short-Run Profit to a Firm

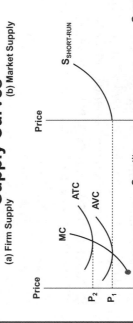

To maximize profit:

MC = MR = Price

Zero profit when:

ATC = Price

Losses when:

ATC > Price

Economic profit:
Total revenue less opportunity cost of production

© Kaplan, Inc.

58 - 3

LOS 16.b,d,e Explain/Describe/Determine
CFAI p. 156 Schweser p. 96

Perfect Competition – Equilibrium

Firm Demand Curve – Perfect Competition

© Kaplan, Inc.

59

LOS 16.c Describe
CFAI p. 173 Schweser p. 114

Firm vs. Industry Short-Run
Supply Curves

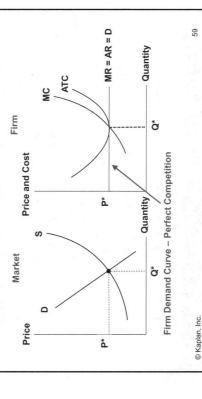

(a) Firm Supply

(b) Market Supply

$S_{SHORT-RUN}$

Price < P_1:
Insufficient to cover fixed or variable cost

$P_1 \leq$ Price < P_2:
Insufficient to cover fixed costs; variable costs covered

Price > P_2:
All costs covered and profit now made

© Kaplan, Inc.

60 - 3

Effects of a Permanent Increase in Demand

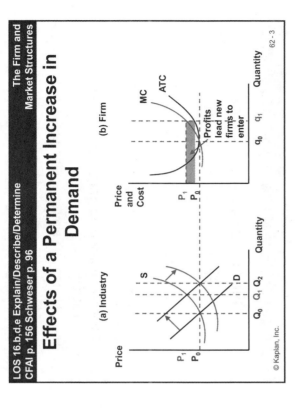

62 - 3

Monopolistic Competition

- A large number of firms in industry:
  - Each firm has a small market share
  - Concerned about average price
  - Collusion not possible
  - Firms produce differentiated products (close but not perfect substitutes)
  - Relatively elastic demand
  - Firms compete on price, quality, and marketing
  - Low barriers to entry

64

Short-Run Increase in Demand

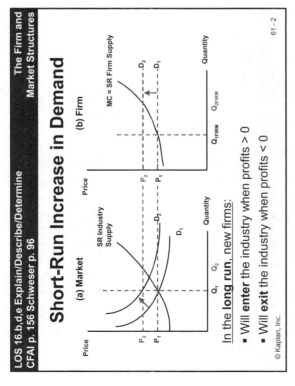

In the **long run**, new firms:

- Will **enter** the industry when profits > 0
- Will **exit** the industry when profits < 0

61 - 2

For Acme Corp., a price taker, the market price of their product permanently falls below ATC but is above AVC and MC. In the short run and long run, Acme should:

	Short Run	Long Run
A.	shut down	shut down
B.	shut down	operate
C.	operate	shut down

63 - 1

Efficiency of Monopolistic Competition

Brand names provide signals about quality

Product innovation and **differentiation** has value to consumers

Advertising provides valuable information to consumers

- High advertising expenditures increase fixed costs and total costs

- If advertising greatly increases sales, ATC can decline because AFC fall

© Kaplan, Inc.   65

Monopolistic Competition

**Short-Run
Output Decision
for a Firm**

**Long-Run
Output Decision
for a Firm**

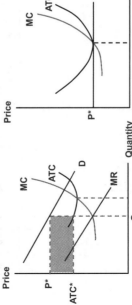

© Kaplan, Inc.   66 - 2

Monopolistic vs. Perfect Competition

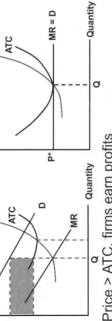

If Price > ATC, firms earn profits

Spending on differentiation and marketing may increase ATC so that ATC = price, no profits

© Kaplan, Inc.   67

Oligopoly Characteristics

- **Small number** of sellers – downward sloping demand

- Firms' demand curve less elastic than monopolistic competition

- **Interdependence** among competitors and their demand curves

- Significant **barriers to entry** (e.g., scale of operations)

  - Products may be similar *or* differentiated

© Kaplan, Inc.   68

Kinked-Demand Model – Oligopoly

Kinked Demand Curve
- Competitors **will not** follow a price increase
- Competitors **will** follow a price decrease
- Model gives a discontinuous marginal revenue curve (gap)
- Model does not specify what determines the market price P_K

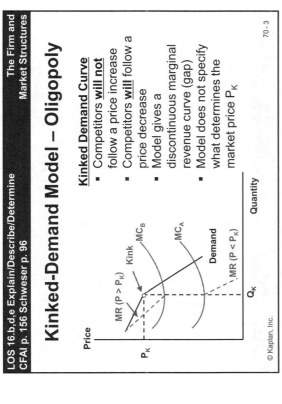

70 - 3

© Kaplan, Inc.

Oligopoly Profits With Collusion

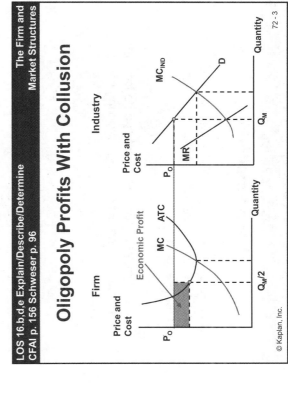

72 - 3

© Kaplan, Inc.

Dominant Firm Oligopoly

- One (dominant) firm is the low cost producer and produces most of the industry output
- Dominant firm **essentially sets market price**
  - Other firms choose output that maximizes profit at the price established by the dominant firm

69

© Kaplan, Inc.

Cournot (duopoly) Model

Assumptions:
- Two firms
- Homogeneous product
- Firms have market power (downward sloping demand)
- Both firms have identical and constant marginal costs of production

Result:
Each firm ends up supplying 1/2 the market

71

© Kaplan, Inc.

Slide 73

Oligopoly and Game Theory

Oligopoly firms can earn a greater profit if they **collude**, fix industry output at the monopoly (profit maximizing) quantity, and share the profits

Game theory suggests that if competitors cannot detect cheating, they will choose to violate the collusion agreement and increase output

© Kaplan, Inc.

73

Slide 74

Nash Equilibrium

Choices of all firms are such that no other choice makes any firm better off (increases profits or decreases losses)

Strategic games model the best choice for a firm depending on the actions and reactions of competitors

© Kaplan, Inc.

74

Slide 75

Nash Equilibrium and Oligopoly

	Firm B honors	Firm B cheats
Firm A honors	A profit = $225m B profit = $225m	A profit = $75m B profit = $300
Firm A cheats	A profit = $300m B profit = $75m	A profit = $150m B profit = $150m

Nash Equilibrium

Collusion will be more successful with:
- Fewer firms
- Homogeneous products
- Similar cost structures
- Certain and severe retaliation for cheating
- Little competition from firms outside the agreement

© Kaplan, Inc.

75 - 3

Slide 76

Monopoly Characteristics

Barriers to entry:
- Economies of scale (natural monopoly)
- Government licensing and legal barriers
- Resource control

A single-price monopolist faces downward sloping demand and must reduce price to increase sales; thus, marginal revenue is less than price

With price discrimination buyers charged different prices (can increase economic efficiency)

© Kaplan, Inc.

76

LOS 16.b,d,e Explain/Describe/Determine
CFAI p. 156 Schweser p. 96

Monopoly Costs, Price, and Revenue

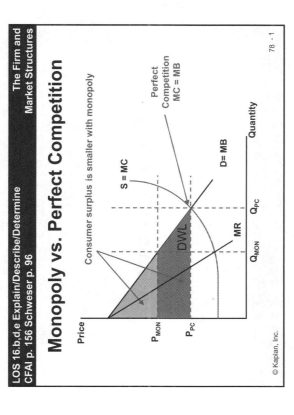

LOS 16.b,d,e Explain/Describe/Determine
CFAI p. 156 Schweser p. 96

Monopoly vs. Perfect Competition

Consumer surplus is smaller with monopoly

Perfect
Competition
MC = MB

S = MC

D = MB

DWL

MR

Price

P_MON

P_PC

Q_MON   Q_PC   Quantity

LOS 16.b,d,e Explain/Describe/Determine
CFAI p. 156 Schweser p. 96

Natural Monopoly

Significant economies of scale

- ATC declines as output increases
- Often high fixed cost industries
- Marginal cost tends to be low
- *Example*: Utilities

LOS 16.c Describe
CFAI p. 173 Schweser p. 114

Firm's Supply Function

Perfect Competition:

- MC curve above average variable cost
- Market supply = sum of supply of market participants

Monopolistic Competition, Oligopoly, Monopoly:

- No well-defined supply function (can't construct quantity supplied as a function of price)
- Supply driven by intersection of MR and MC; price is then determined by quantity and the demand curve

Pricing Strategy

- **Perfect Competition:** Price = MR = MC at profit maximizing output quantity

- **Monopoly, Monopolistic Competition:** MR = MC at profit maximizing output quantity; price determined by downward-sloping demand curve; P > MR

- **Oligopoly:** Optimal pricing strategy depends on how other firms are expected to react
  - Cournot Duopoly
  - Kinked demand curve
  - Dominant firm
  - Game theory, Collusion

© Kaplan, Inc.

81

Concentration Measures

N-Firm Concentration Ratio: Sum of the percentage market shares of the *N* largest firms in an industry

Advantage: Simple

Limitations: Ignores barriers to entry, largely unaffected by mergers

Herfindahl-Hirschman Index (HHI): Sum of squared market shares of *N* largest firms in a market

Advantages: More sensitive to mergers than *N*-firm ratio, widely used by regulators

Limitations: Ignores barriers to entry, ignores elasticity of demand

© Kaplan, Inc.

82

Additional Problems

A market where individual producers face downward sloping demand, barriers to entry are low, and producer pricing decisions are not directly affected by decisions of other producers is referred to as:

A. an oligopoly.

B. perfect competition.

C. monopolistic competition.

© Kaplan, Inc.

83 - 1

Additional Problems

1) A firm uses labor inputs with a cost of $45 per unit of labor and a marginal product of 15 units of output. The firm uses capital inputs with a cost of $60 per unit of capital and a marginal product of 20 units of output. Is this firm minimizing its cost per unit of output?

A. Yes.

B. No, the firm should use more labor and less capital.

C. No, the firm should use more capital and less labor.

-4

Additional Problems

2) A Giffen good is *best* described as a(n):

A. inferior good for which a decrease in price will decrease quantity demanded.

B. normal good for which an increase in price will increase quantity demanded.

C. inferior good for which a decrease in price will increase quantity demanded.

-1

CFA Curriculum Vol. 2,
R.16, Q.18, p. 201

3) In an industry comprised of three companies, which are small-scale manufacturers of an easily replicable product unprotected by brand recognition or patents, the *most* representative model of company behavior is:

A. oligopoly.

B. perfect competition.

C. monopolistic competition.

-1

CFA Curriculum Vol. 2,
R.16, Q.17, p. 200

4) One disadvantage of the Herfindahl-Hirschmann Index is that the index:

A. is difficult to compute.

B. fails to reflect low barriers to entry.

C. fails to reflect the effect of mergers in the industry.

-1

STUDY SESSION 4 ANSWERS

Reading	Slide Number	Answer
13	13	B
13	16	C
13	18	C
14	35	A
15	47	A
15	54	B
16	63	C
16	83	C

Additional Problems

1. A

2. A

3. B

4. B

Study Session 5

Economics: Macroeconomic Analysis

Economics: Macroeconomic Analysis

17. Aggregate Output, Prices, and Economic Growth

KAPLAN UNIVERSITY | SCHOOL OF PROFESSIONAL AND CONTINUING EDUCATION | SCHWESER

Study Session 5
Economics: Macroeconomic Analysis

17. Aggregate Output, Prices, and Economic Growth
18. Understanding Business Cycles
19. Monetary and Fiscal Policy

KAPLAN UNIVERSITY | SCHOOL OF PROFESSIONAL AND CONTINUING EDUCATION | SCHWESER

LOS 17.a Calculate/Explain
CFAI p. 210, Schweser p. 126

Calculating GDP
Income Approach

Earnings of all households + businesses + government

Expenditures Approach

Sum the market values of all final goods and services produced in the economy

OR

Sum all the increases in value at each stage of the production process

---

LOS 17.a Calculate/Explain
CFAI p. 210, Schweser p. 126

Gross Domestic Product (GDP)

Market value of all final goods and services produced in a country/economy.

- Produced during the period
- Only goods that are valued in the market
- Final goods and services only (not intermediate)
- Rental value for owner-occupied housing (estimated)
- Government services (at cost)—not transfers

GDP: Expenditures Approach

GDP = C + I + G + (X – M)

C = consumption spending

I = business investment (capital equipment + change in inventories)

G = government purchases

X = exports

M = imports

© Kaplan, Inc.   4

Nominal vs. Real GDP

Nominal GDP

Sum of all current-year goods and services at current-year prices.

$$\sum Q_t \times P_t$$

Real GDP (measures increase in physical output)

Sum of all current year goods and services at base-year prices.

With base year = t – 5: $\sum Q_t \times P_{t-5}$

© Kaplan, Inc.   5

GDP Deflator

$$GDP\ Deflator = \frac{Nominal\ GDP}{Real\ GDP} \times 100$$

With base year t – 5, a GDP deflator of 112.3 means prices have gone up by 12.3% over 5 years—a measure of inflation

$$Real\ GDP = \frac{Nominal\ GDP}{GDP\ Deflator} \times 100 = \frac{Nominal\ GDP}{\left(\frac{GDP\ Deflator}{100}\right)}$$

© Kaplan, Inc.   6

National Income

GDP = **national income**

  + capital consumption allowance

  + statistical discrepancy

Capital consumption allowance is the output that goes to replace capital stock wearing out, depreciation

© Kaplan, Inc.   7

LOS 17.d Compare
CFAI p. 221, Schweser p. 129

National Income

National income

= employees' wages and benefits

+ corporate and government profits pre-tax

+ interest income

+ unincorporated business owners' income

+ rent

+ indirect business taxes – subsidies

(taxes and subsidies included in final prices)

© Kaplan, Inc.

8

LOS 17.d Compare
CFAI p. 221, Schweser p. 129

Personal Income

Personal income

= national income

+ transfer payments to households

– indirect business taxes

– corporate income taxes

– undistributed corporate profits

© Kaplan, Inc.

9

LOS 17.d Compare
CFAI p. 221, Schweser p. 129

Personal Disposable Income

Personal disposable income

= personal income – personal taxes

= **after-tax income**

Each period, individuals decide whether to consume or save disposable income

© Kaplan, Inc.

10

In the income-based approach to calculating gross domestic product, the difference between national income and gross domestic product is:

A. depreciation.

B. corporate income taxes.

C. transfer payments from government to individuals.

© Kaplan, Inc.

11- 1

Slide 12-1

Aggregate Output, Prices,
and Economic Growth

The GDP deflator is calculated as 100 times:

A. $\dfrac{\text{current year nominal GDP}}{\text{base year nominal GDP}}$

B. $\dfrac{\text{base year output at current year prices}}{\text{base year nominal GDP}}$

C. $\dfrac{\text{current year nominal GDP}}{\text{current year output at base year prices}}$

© Kaplan, Inc.

12-1

Slide 13-3

Aggregate Output, Prices,
and Economic Growth

LOS 17.e Explain
CFAI p. 227, Schweser p. 130

Deriving the Fundamental Relationship

$\text{GDP} = C + I + G + (X - M)$ **Total Expenditures**

$\text{GDP} = C + S + T$ **Total Income**

$\cancel{C} + S + T = \cancel{C} + I + G + (X - M)$

$S + T = I + G + (X - M)$

$S = I + (G - T) + (X - M)$

© Kaplan, Inc.

13-3

Slide 14

Aggregate Output, Prices,
and Economic Growth

LOS 17.e Explain
CFAI p. 227, Schweser p. 130

Fundamental Relationship

$$S = I + (G - T) + (X - M)$$

Savings = Investment + Fiscal Balance + Trade Balance

Savings are either invested, used to finance government deficit, or used to fund a trade surplus, when both exist

© Kaplan, Inc.

14

Slide 15

Aggregate Output, Prices,
and Economic Growth

LOS 17.f Explain
CFAI p. 227, Schweser p. 131

The Income = Savings (IS) Curve

When income = planned expenditure:
$$(S - I) = (G - T) + (X - M)$$

Increase in real interest rate, holding $(G - T) + (X - M)$ and $(S - I)$ constant:

- Investment decreases
- Savings must also decrease
- Decrease in savings must result from decrease in income

© Kaplan, Inc.

15

LOS 17.f Explain
Aggregate Output, Prices, and Economic Growth
CFAI p. 227, Schweser p. 131

Equilibrium in the Money Market

Real money supply (M/P)

Money demand = f (real rates, income)

$$M/P = MD\ (r, Y)$$

Real rates up → quantity demanded ↓
Income up → quantity demanded ↑

Higher real interest rates → higher income

© Kaplan, Inc.   17

LOS 17.f Explain
Aggregate Output, Prices, and Economic Growth
CFAI p. 227, Schweser p. 131

The Aggregate Demand Curve

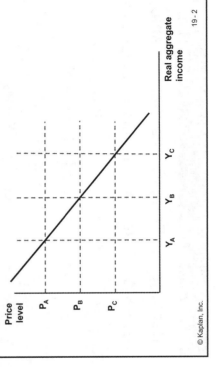

© Kaplan, Inc.   19 - 2

LOS 17.f Explain
Aggregate Output, Prices, and Economic Growth
CFAI p. 227, Schweser p. 131

The IS Curve

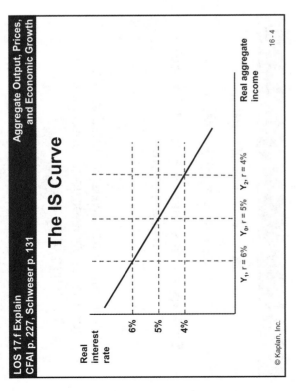

© Kaplan, Inc.   16 - 4

LOS 17.f Explain
Aggregate Output, Prices, and Economic Growth
CFAI p. 227, Schweser p. 131

The LM Curve

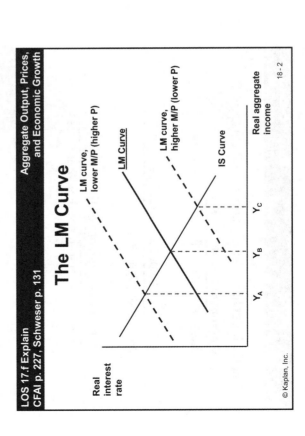

© Kaplan, Inc.   18 - 2

Equilibrium in the Money Market

Real money supply (M/P)

Money demand = f (real rates, income)

$$M/P = MD \ (r, Y)$$

Real rates up → quantity demanded ↓

Income up → quantity demanded ↑

Higher real interest rates → higher income

20

An increase in the price level would shift the:

A. IS curve.

B. LM curve.

C. aggregate demand curve.

22 - 1

An increase in the nominal money supply would shift the:

A. IS curve and the LM curve.

B. IS curve and the aggregate demand curve.

C. LM curve and the aggregate demand curve.

21 - 1

Aggregate Supply

- In the **very short run**: Aggregate supply is elastic (input prices are fixed)

  - In the **short run**: Input prices are fixed so businesses expand real output when (output) prices increase

  - In the **long run**: Aggregate supply is fixed at full-employment or potential real GDP

23

Aggregate Supply

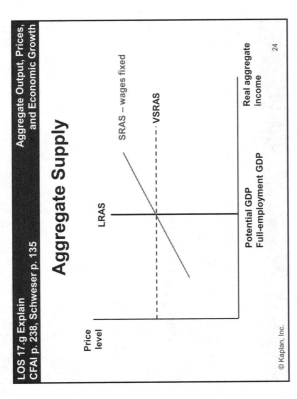

© Kaplan, Inc.

24

Aggregate Demand

The **aggregate demand curve (AD)** shows the relation between the price level and the real quantity of final goods and services (real GDP) demanded

Components of aggregate demand

- Consumption (C)
- Investment (I)
- Government spending (G)
- Net exports (X), exports minus imports

Aggregate demand = $C + I + G +_{net}X$

© Kaplan, Inc.

25

Shifts in Aggregate Demand

$C + I + G + netX$

Increases in wealth increase C

Increases in expectations for economic growth increase C, I

Capacity utilization > ~85% → increases I

Increases in tax rates decrease disposable income and C

© Kaplan, Inc.

26

Shifts in Aggregate Demand

$C + I + G + netX$

Increases in government spending, G

Increases in the money supply reduce real rates and increase I, C

Depreciation of currency increases netX, imports prices up, export prices down

Growth of foreign GDP increases netX

© Kaplan, Inc.

27

Shifts in SR Aggregate Supply

LOS 17.h Explain
CFAI p. 240, Schweser p. 136

Aggregate Output, Prices,
and Economic Growth

Factors that Increase SRAS

1. Decreases in input prices

2. Improved expectations about future

3. Decreases in business taxes

4. Increases in business subsidies

5. Currency appreciation that reduces the cost of imported inputs

© Kaplan, Inc.

28

Shifts in LR Aggregate Supply

LOS 17.h Explain
CFAI p. 240, Schweser p. 136

Aggregate Output, Prices,
and Economic Growth

Factors that Increase LRAS

- Increase in labor supply
- Increased availability of natural resources
- Increased stock of physical capital
- Increased human capital (labor quality)
- Advances in technology/labor productivity

© Kaplan, Inc.

29

Increase in Aggregate Demand

LOS 17.i,j,k Describe/Distinguish/Explain
CFAI p. 253, Schweser p. 140

Aggregate Output, Prices,
and Economic Growth

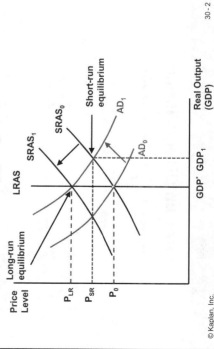

© Kaplan, Inc.

30 - 2

Decrease in Aggregate Demand

LOS 17.i,j,k Describe/Distinguish/Explain
CFAI p. 253, Schweser p. 140

Aggregate Output, Prices,
and Economic Growth

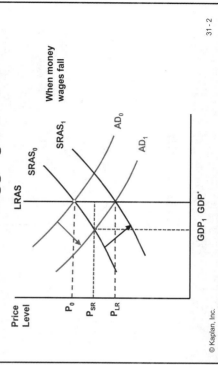

© Kaplan, Inc.

31 - 2

Short-Run Disequilibrium

Below full employment   **Above full employment**

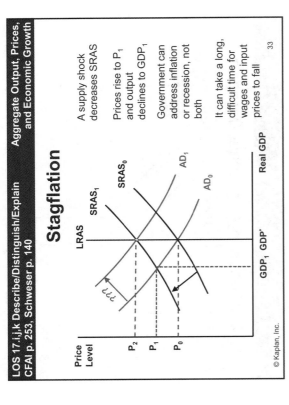

Stagflation

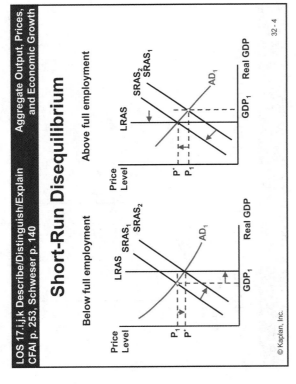

A supply shock
decreases SRAS

Prices rise to P_1
and output
declines to GDP_1

Government can
address inflation
or recession, not
both

It can take a long,
difficult time for
wages and input
prices to fall

Sources of Economic Growth

Same as factors that increase LRAS

1. Increase in labor supply

2. Increased availability of natural resources

3. Increased stock of physical capital

4. Increased human capital (labor quality)

5. Advances in technology/labor productivity

Sustainable Growth

Potential GDP =

Aggregate hours worked × labor productivity

Growth in Potential GDP =

growth in labor force +

growth in labor productivity

**Long-term equity returns are dependent on
sustainable growth**

Aggregate Output, Prices,
and Economic Growth

Production Function Approach

$$Y = A \times f(L, K)$$

where:

Y = aggregate economic output

L = size of labor force

K = amount of capital available

A = total factor productivity, the increase in output not from increases in labor and capital, closely related to advances in technology

© Kaplan, Inc.   36

Aggregate Output, Prices,
and Economic Growth

Components of Economic Growth

Growth in potential GDP =

growth in total factor productivity +

W_C (growth in capital) +

W_L (growth in labor)

Where the weights are each factor's share of national income

© Kaplan, Inc.   37

Aggregate Output, Prices,
and Economic Growth

Per Capita Growth

Growth in per-capita potential GDP =

growth in technology +

W_C(growth in the capital-to-labor ratio)

In developed countries, K/L is high and growth in per capital GDP must come from technological advancement.

© Kaplan, Inc.   38

Aggregate Output, Prices,
and Economic Growth

Growth of potential GDP has been 7% and labor's share of national income is 70%. The increase in the labor force has been 6% and the increase in the capital stock has been 5%. What is the increase in total factor productivity over the period?

© Kaplan, Inc.   39 - 2

Demand and Supply Analysis: Introduction

Additional LOS

LOS 17.b: methods of calculating GDP

LOS 17.o: input growth and total factor productivity

41

© Kaplan, Inc.

Aggregate Output, Prices, and Economic Growth

When the economy is operating at full-employment GDP, the short-run and long-run effects of an increase in the rate of growth of the money supply are to:

A. decrease real interest rates in the short run and increase real GDP in the long run.

B. increase real GDP in the short run but not in the long run.

C. increase the price level and real GDP in both the short and long run.

40 - 1

© Kaplan, Inc.

Understanding Business Cycles

LOS 18.a Describe
CFAI p. 290, Schweser p. 157

Business Cycles

Cyclical behavior of GDP growth, inflation, and employment

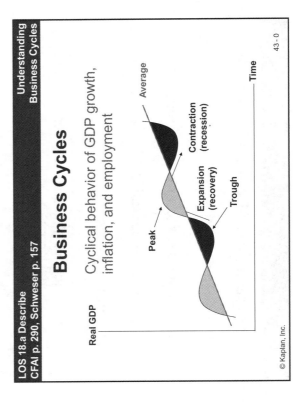

43 - 0

© Kaplan, Inc.

Economics

Economics: Macroeconomic Analysis

18. Understanding Business Cycles

KAPLAN UNIVERSITY   SCHOOL OF PROFESSIONAL AND CONTINUING EDUCATION | SCHWESER

Based on typical labor utilization patterns across the business cycle, productivity (output per hours worked) is *most likely* to be highest:

A. at the peak of a boom.

B. into a maturing expansion

C. at the bottom of a recession.

44 - 1

Business Cycle Theories

School of Thought	Cause of Business Cycles	Recommended Policy
Neoclassical	Technology changes	Allow wages, prices to adjust
Keynesian	AD shifts with changes in business expectations; contractions persist due to downward sticky wages	Use fiscal and/or monetary policy to restore full employment
New Keynesian	Same as Keynesian; but other input prices also downward sticky	Same as Keynesian

© Kaplan, Inc.

45

Business Cycle Theories

School of Thought	Cause of Business Cycles	Recommended Policy
Monetarist	Inappropriate changes in money supply growth rate	Steady, predictable growth rate of money supply
Austrian	Government intervention in economy	Don't force interest rates to artificially low levels
New Classical (Real Business Cycle theory)	Rational responses to external shocks, technology changes	Don't intervene to counteract business cycles

© Kaplan, Inc.

46

Types of Unemployment

- **Frictional** unemployment results from time it takes employers and employees to find each other

- **Structural** unemployment results from long-term changes in the economy that require workers to gain new skills to fill new jobs

- **Cyclical** unemployment results from changes in economic growth; equals zero at full employment

© Kaplan, Inc.

47

Understanding Business Cycles

LOS 18.d Describe
CFAI p. 313, Schweser p. 162

Employment Measures

- To be unemployed, must be available for work and actively looking for work

- Labor force consists of those who are employed and those who are unemployed

- Unemployment rate = $\dfrac{\text{Number of unemployed}}{\text{Labor force}}$

- Participation ratio = $\dfrac{\text{Labor force}}{\text{Working-age population (>16)}}$

- Discouraged workers not employed or seeking employment; **not counted in labor force**

© Kaplan, Inc.

48

Understanding Business Cycles

LOS 18.e Explain
CFAI p. 317, Schweser p. 163

Inflation, Disinflation, and Deflation

- **Inflation:** Persistent increase in price level over time

- **Inflation rate:** Percent increase in price level over a period (usually one year)

- **Disinflation:** Decrease in positive inflation rate over time

- **Deflation:** Persistent decrease in price level over time; negative inflation rate

- **Hyperinflation:** Out-of-control high inflation

© Kaplan, Inc.

49

Understanding Business Cycles

LOS 18.f Explain
CFAI p. 319, Schweser p. 164

Calculating the CPI

1. Find the cost of the CPI basket in the base period

2. Find the cost of the CPI basket in the current period

3. Calculate the price index:

$$CPI = \dfrac{\text{cost of basket at current prices}}{\text{cost of basket at base year prices}} \times 100$$

Example: $CPI = \dfrac{\$2,900}{\$2,500} \times 100 = 116$

Prices up 16% over the period

© Kaplan, Inc.

50

Understanding Business Cycles

LOS 18.f,g Explain/Compare
CFAI p. 319, Schweser p. 164

Headline and Core Inflation

- Price indexes that include all goods and services measure **headline inflation**

- **Core inflation** refers to prices of all goods excluding food and energy

- Food and energy prices are subject to large short-term fluctuations that can magnify or mask the true inflation rate

© Kaplan, Inc.

51

Limitations of Inflation Measures

The CPI is widely believed to **overstate** the true rate of inflation

The most significant biases in the CPI data include:

- Consumer **substitution** of lower-priced products for higher-priced products

- **New goods** replace older, lower-priced products

- Price increases due to **quality improvements**

© Kaplan, Inc.   52

Adjustments for CPI Bias

- CPI is calculated using basket weights from base period (Laspeyres index)

- A Paasche index uses basket weights from current period and compares cost to base period

- **Chained price index** reduces bias from substitution

  (e.g., Fisher index = geometric mean of Laspeyres and Paasche indexes)

© Kaplan, Inc.   53

Cost-Push Inflation (SRAS down)

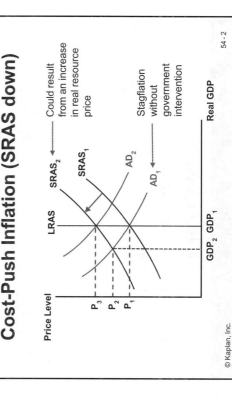

© Kaplan, Inc.   54 - 2

Demand-Pull Inflation (AD up)

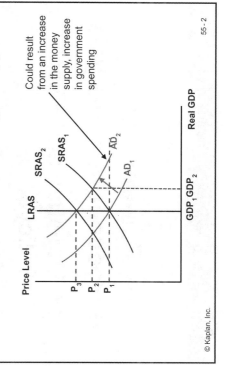

© Kaplan, Inc.   55 - 2

Economics: Macroeconomic Analysis
19. Monetary and Fiscal Policy

KAPLAN UNIVERSITY — SCHOOL OF PROFESSIONAL AND CONTINUING EDUCATION | SCHWESER

© Kaplan, Inc.

LOS 19.a Compare
CFAI p. 347, Schweser p. 179

Fiscal Policy

- **Government decisions on taxing and spending**

- **Expansionary:** Increase spending and/or decrease taxes; increase the budget deficit, increase aggregate demand

- **Contractionary:** Decrease spending and/or increase taxes; decrease the budget deficit, reduce aggregate demand

© Kaplan, Inc.

59

Additional LOS

LOS 18.i: uses and limitations of economic indicators

© Kaplan, Inc.

56

LOS 19.a Compare
CFAI p. 347, Schweser p. 179

Monetary Policy

Management of the supply of money and credit

Expansionary: Increase the money supply, decrease interest rates, increase aggregate demand

Contractionary: Decrease the money supply, increase interest rates, slow economic growth and inflation

© Kaplan, Inc.

58

LOS 19.d Describe
CFAI p. 355, Schweser p. 182   Monetary and Fiscal Policy

Equilibrium in the Money Market

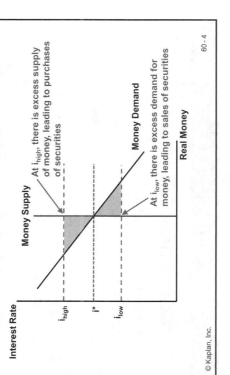

Interest Rate

Money Supply

At i_{high}, there is excess supply of money, leading to purchases of securities

Money Demand

At i_{low}, there is excess demand for money, leading to sales of securities

i_{high}

i^*

i_{low}

Real Money

© Kaplan, Inc.   60 - 4

LOS 19.e Describe
CFAI p. 358, Schweser p. 184   Monetary and Fiscal Policy

Fisher Effect

**Riskless nominal interest rate =
real riskless rate + expected inflation**

There is also uncertainty about future inflation rates and other economic variables, and a risk premium that increases with uncertainty

**Riskless nominal interest rate =
real riskless rate + expected inflation
+ risk premium for uncertainty**

© Kaplan, Inc.   61

LOS 19.f Describe
CFAI p. 361, Schweser p. 184   Monetary and Fiscal Policy

Objectives of Central Banks

All central banks have price stability (low inflation rates) as an objective. Many (except U.S. and Japan) have explicit target rates, usually 2% to 3%.

Some central banks also attempt to:

- Maintain full employment
- Promote economic growth
- Keep exchange rates stable
- Keep long-term interest rates moderate

© Kaplan, Inc.   62

LOS 19.h Describe
CFAI p. 367, Schweser p. 187   Monetary and Fiscal Policy

Monetary Policy Tools

<u>Policy rate</u>: Interest rate central banks charge banks for borrowed reserves

- By raising the policy rate, Fed discourages banks from borrowing reserves; thus, they reduce their lending
  - Decreasing the discount rate tends to increase the amount of lending and the money supply
  - The U.S. Fed sets a target for the fed funds rate, the rate at which banks lend short-term to each other

© Kaplan, Inc.   63

Monetary Policy Tools

Open market operations: *Most often used*

- Central bank buys government securities for cash, reserves increase, money supply increases

- Selling securities decreases the money supply

Required reserve ratio: *Seldom changed*

- Reducing required reserve percentage increases excess reserves and increases the money supply

- Increasing required reserve ratio decreases the money supply

© Kaplan, Inc.   64

Monetary Policy Transmission

Expansionary monetary policy affects four things:

1. Market interest rates fall, less incentive to save

2. Asset prices increase, wealth effect, consumption spending increases

3. Expectations for economic growth increase, may expect further decreases in interest rates

4. Domestic currency depreciates, import prices increase, export prices decrease

   Overall, aggregate demand increases, increasing real GDP, employment, and inflation

© Kaplan, Inc.   65

Central Bank Characteristics

To be **effective**, central banks should be:

1. **Independent**—free from political interference

   Not absolute; viewed as degree of independence

2. **Credible**: Bank follows through on stated intentions and policies

3. **Transparent:** Bank discloses inflation reports, indicators they use, and how they use them

© Kaplan, Inc.   66

Monetary Policy Effects on Economy

When a central bank buys securities:

- Bank reserves increase

- Interbank lending rates decrease

- Short-term and long-term lending rates decrease

- Businesses increase investment

- Consumers increase house, auto, and durable goods purchases

- Domestic currency depreciates, exports increase

  Overall, aggregate demand increases, increasing real GDP, employment, and inflation

© Kaplan, Inc.   67

LOS 19.l Contrast
CFAI p. 371, Schweser p. 190   Monetary and Fiscal Policy

Central Bank Targets

- **Interest rate targeting:** Increase (decrease) money supply growth when interest rates are above (below) targets

- **Inflation targeting:** Target band for inflation rate (typically 1% to 3%), inflation band > 0 to prevent deflation

- **Exchange rate targeting:** Target band for currency exchange rate with developed country Results in same inflation rate in domestic economy as in targeted developed country

© Kaplan, Inc.   68

LOS 19.m Describe
CFAI p. 380, Schweser p. 191   Monetary and Fiscal Policy

The Neutral Interest Rate

Neutral interest rate = trend growth rate of real GDP + target inflation rate

Policy rate > neutral rate: <u>Contractionary</u>

Policy rate < neutral rate: <u>Expansionary</u>

© Kaplan, Inc.   69

CFA Curriculum Vol. 2,
R.19, Q.21, p. 413   Monetary and Fiscal Policy

Which of the following is a limitation on the ability of central banks to stimulate growth in periods of deflation?

A. Ricardian equivalence.

B. The interaction of monetary and fiscal policy.

C. The fact that interest rates have a minimum value (0%).

70 - 1

CFA Curriculum Vol. 2,
R.19, Q.22, p. 413   Monetary and Fiscal Policy

The *least likely* limitation to the effectiveness of monetary policy is that central banks cannot:

A. accurately determine the neutral rate of interest.

B. regulate the willingness of financial institutions to lend.

C. control amounts that economic agents deposit into banks.

71 - 1

Fiscal Policy

Expansionary Fiscal Policy

Increase government spending, decrease taxes, or both—increasing aggregate demand and the budget deficit

Contractionary Fiscal Policy

Decrease government spending, increase taxes, or both—decreasing aggregate demand and the budget deficit

© Kaplan, Inc.

72

Fiscal Policy

- **Keynesian economists** believe **discretionary fiscal policy** can stabilize the economy, increasing aggregate demand to combat recessions and decreasing aggregate demand to combat inflation

- **Monetarists** believe that such effects are temporary and that appropriate monetary policy will dampen economic cycles

- **Automatic stabilizers** (taxes and transfer payments) tend to increase deficits during recessions and decrease deficits during expansions

© Kaplan, Inc.

73

Fiscal Policy Tools: Spending

1. **Transfer payments**: Cash payments by government to redistribute wealth

2. **Current spending**: Purchases of goods and services

3. **Capital spending**: To increase future productivity; on infrastructure, or to support research on and development of new technologies

© Kaplan, Inc.

74

Fiscal Policy Tools: Revenue

Direct taxes—levied on income or wealth

  Take time to implement

Indirect taxes—levied on goods and services

  Quick to implement to raise revenue or promote social goals (e.g., tobacco tax)

© Kaplan, Inc.

75

LOS 19.p Describe
CFAI p. 394, Schweser p. 194   Monetary and Fiscal Policy

Fiscal Multiplier

Initial government spending has a multiplied effect as it creates more spending

Government purchases multiplier $= \dfrac{1}{1 - MPC(1-t)}$

↑savings and ↑tax rate reduce the multiplier

For MPC = 0.8 and t = 0.3, a $100 billion spending increase, over time, can increase consumption by
$1 / [1 - 0.8(1 - 0.3)] \times \$100 = \$227$ billion

76

© Kaplan, Inc.

LOS 19.p Describe
CFAI p. 394, Schweser p. 194   Monetary and Fiscal Policy

Tax Multiplier

- With MPC = 0.8, a tax increase of $100 billion will reduce consumption by = $0.8 \times 100 = \$80$ billion
  - The fiscal multiplier effect will, over time, lead to a <u>decrease</u> in consumption spending of $2.27 \times \$80$ billion = $182 billion

The **balanced budget multiplier** is positive

A $100 billion increase in spending + a $100 billion increase in taxes can, over time, increase consumption spending by $227 − $182 = $45 billion

77

© Kaplan, Inc.

LOS 19.p Describe
CFAI p. 394, Schweser p. 194   Monetary and Fiscal Policy

Ricardian Equivalence

- If a tax decrease causes taxpayers to increase savings in anticipation of higher future taxes, the resulting decrease in spending will reduce the expansionary impact of a tax cut

- If the increase in saving (decrease in consumption) just offsets the tax decrease, it is termed **Ricardian equivalence**

- An increase in spending funded by issuing debt will have no impact on aggregate demand

78

© Kaplan, Inc.

LOS 19.r Explain
CFAI p. 400, Schweser p. 198   Monetary and Fiscal Policy

Fiscal Policy Lags

Recognition lag: To identify the need for fiscal policy change

Action lag: To enact legislation

Impact lag: For the policy change to have the intended effect

Lags can cause fiscal policy changes to be destabilizing rather than stabilizing

79

© Kaplan, Inc.

LOS 19.r Explain
CFAI p. 400, Schweser p. 198   Monetary and Fiscal Policy

Fiscal Policy Limitations

- If economy is at full employment, fiscal stimulus will result in higher inflation

- If economy is below full employment due to supply shortages, fiscal stimulus will lead to inflation rather than GDP growth

- If the economy has high unemployment and high inflation (stagflation), fiscal policy cannot address both

© Kaplan, Inc.

80

LOS 19.s Determine
CFAI p. 386, Schweser p. 199   Monetary and Fiscal Policy

Analysis of Fiscal Policy

- Whether fiscal policy is expansionary or contractionary depends on the business cycle stage

- An adjusted, or full-employment, deficit amount can be used to adjust for the business cycle stage

In general:

Spending increases, tax decreases—**expansionary**

Spending decreases, tax increases—**contractionary**

© Kaplan, Inc.

81

LOS 19.t Explain
CFAI p. 404, Schweser p. 200   Monetary and Fiscal Policy

Policy Interaction

- **Monetary ↑ and Fiscal ↑:** Strong expansionary effect, public and private sectors grow

- **Monetary ↓ and Fiscal ↓:** Decreased GDP growth, higher interest rates, public and private sectors decline

- **Monetary ↑ and Fiscal ↓:** Interest rates fall, consumption, output, and private sector expand

- **Monetary ↓ and Fiscal ↑:** Interest rates rise, aggregate demand likely higher, public sector portion of spending grows

© Kaplan, Inc.

82

Monetary and Fiscal Policy

The balanced budget multiplier is positive because:

A. the tax multiplier effect is stronger than the government purchases multiplier effect.

B. the government purchases multiplier effect is stronger than the tax multiplier effect.

C. The negative effect of the government purchases multiplier is less than the positive effect of the tax multiplier.

© Kaplan, Inc.

83 - 2

Additional LOS

The *most likely* argument against high national debt levels is that:

A. the debt is owed internally to fellow citizens.

B. they create disincentives for economic activity.

C. they may finance investment in physical and human capital.

84 - 1

Monetary and Fiscal Policy

Additional LOS

LOS 19.b: functions and definitions of money

LOS 19.c: money creation process

LOS 19.g: expected and unexpected inflation

85

Economics

Additional Problems

Additional Problems

1) Limitations on the ability of expansionary fiscal policy to increase real GDP *least likely* include:

A. resource constraints.

B. reduced consumption due to increased taxes.

C. reduced private investment due to government borrowing.

- 1

Additional Problems

2) The fundamental relationship between saving (S), investment (I), the fiscal balance (G –T), and the trade balance (X – M) is *best* represented by:

A. $S = I + (G - T) + (X - M)$.

B. $(X - M) = I - S - (G - T)$.

C. $(G - T) = (S - I) + (X - M)$.

5-1

STUDY SESSION 5 ANSWERS

Reading	Slide Number	Answer
17	11	A
17	12	C
17	21	C
17	22	B
17	39	$\Delta\text{TFP} = 1.3\%$
17	40	B
18	44	C
19	70	C
19	71	A
19	83	B
19	84	B

Additional Problems

1. B

2. A

Study Session 6

Economics: Economics in a Global Context

Economics: Economics in a Global Context

20. International Trade and Capital Flows

KAPLAN UNIVERSITY | SCHOOL OF PROFESSIONAL AND CONTINUING EDUCATION | SCHWESER

Study Session 6
Economics: Economics in a Global Context

20. International Trade and Capital Flows
21. Currency Exchange Rates

KAPLAN UNIVERSITY | SCHOOL OF PROFESSIONAL AND CONTINUING EDUCATION | SCHWESER

LOS 20.b Describe
CFAI p.429, Schweser p. 211

Benefits/Costs of International Trade

Benefits:

- Lower cost to consumers of imports
- Higher employment, wages, and profits in export industries

Costs:

Displacement of workers and lost profits in industries competing with imported goods

Economists: Benefits outweigh costs

© Kaplan, Inc.

3

LOS 20.a Compare
CFAI p.422, Schweser p. 211

Gross National Product (GNP) and Gross Domestic Product (GDP)

GDP is better for measuring domestic activity

GDP: Value of goods and services produced in a country

GNP: Value of goods and services produced by a country's citizens

Differences:

- Income of citizens working abroad, non-citizens working in country
- Income to capital owned by foreigners, foreign capital owned by citizens

© Kaplan, Inc.

2-1

Slide 4

Absolute vs. Comparative Advantage

Absolute advantage refers to lower cost in terms of resources used

Comparative advantage refers to the lowest *opportunity cost* to produce a product

Law of comparative advantage:

- Trade makes **all countries better off**
- Each country specializes in goods they produce most efficiently and trades for other goods

Outcome: Increased worldwide output and wealth with no country being worse off

© Kaplan, Inc.

Slide 5

Absolute vs. Comparative Advantage

Labor costs per unit produced	Cloth	Wine
England	100	110
Portugal	90	80

Portugal has absolute advantage in both wine and cloth

England has comparative advantage in cloth, opportunity cost of cloth is 10/11 wine in England vs. 9/8 wine in Portugal

Portugal has comparative advantage in wine, opportunity cost of wine is 8/9 cloth in Portugal vs. 11/10 in England

© Kaplan, Inc.

5

Slide 6

Absolute vs. Comparative Advantage

Labor costs per unit produced	Cloth	Wine
England	100	110
Portugal	90	80

- If Portugal specializes in wine production and England specializes in cloth production, both can be better off
- Trade can also produce benefits from economies of scale and efficiencies resulting from cross-border competition

© Kaplan, Inc.

6

Slide 7

Models of Trade

Ricardian model

- Labor is the only factor of production
- Comparative advantage depends on relative labor productivity for different goods

Heckscher-Ohlin model

- Two factors of production: capital and labor
- Comparative advantage depends on relative amount of each factor possessed by a country

© Kaplan, Inc.

7

Heckscher-Ohlin Model

- Under Heckscher-Ohlin model, there is a redistribution of wealth between the two factors of production due to international trade

  - The price of more abundant resource will increase as more of it is used to produce exports

  - Results in a wealth transfer within a country from scarce resource to abundant resource

© Kaplan, Inc.

8

Trade Restrictions

Tariff is a tax imposed on imported goods

Quota is a limitation on the quantity of goods imported

Export subsidies are payments by government to domestic exporters

Minimum domestic content specifies required proportion of product content to be sourced domestically

Voluntary export restraints (VERs) are agreements by exporting countries to limit the quantity of goods they will export to an importing country

© Kaplan, Inc.

9

Effects of Tariffs and Quotas

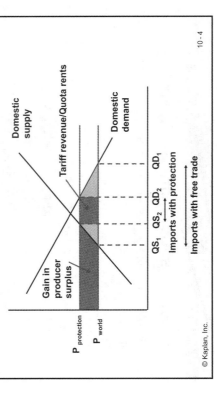

© Kaplan, Inc.

10 - 4

Reasons for Trade Restrictions

Two primary goals:

1. Protecting domestic jobs
2. Protecting domestic producers

- Other reasons include countering foreign trade restrictions and export subsidies, anti-dumping, and revenues from tariff for domestic government

  - A large country could actually decrease the world price by imposing a quota or tariff

© Kaplan, Inc.

11

Slide 12

LOS 20.e Compare
CFAI p.440, Schweser p. 216

Trade Restrictions

Trade Restriction	Domestic Consumer	Domestic Producer	Domestic Government	Foreign Exporter
Tariff	Loses	Gains	Gains	Loses
Quota	Loses	Gains	Gains[1]	Gains[1]
VER	Loses	Gains	None	Gains
Export Subsidy	Loses	Gains	Loses	NA

1. In case of quotas, the distribution of gains between the domestic government and foreign exporter depends on the amount of **quota rent** collected by the domestic government

© Kaplan, Inc.

12

Slide 13

LOS 20.e Compare
CFAI p.440, Schweser p. 216

Capital Restrictions

Restrictions on flow of financial capital

- Outright prohibition
- Punitive taxation
- Restrictions on repatriation

Restrictions decrease economic welfare

Short-term benefit for developing countries: reducing volatile capital inflows and outflows

Long-term costs: isolation from global capital markets

© Kaplan, Inc.

13

Slide 14

LOS 20.g Describe
CFAI p.452, Schweser p. 221

Objectives of Capital Restrictions

- **Reduce volatility** of domestic asset prices due to large inflows and outflows of capital
- **Maintain exchange rate target** while using monetary and fiscal policy for domestic goals
- **Keep domestic interest rates low** by restricting outflows of capital to higher-yielding foreign investments
- **Protect strategic industries** (e.g., defense) from foreign ownership

© Kaplan, Inc.

14

Slide 15

LOS 20.h Describe
CFAI p.455, Schweser p. 221

Balance of Payments (BOP) Accounts

Current Account

Merchandise/services purchases, foreign dividends and interest, and unilateral transfers

Capital Account

Sales/purchases of physical assets, natural resources, intangible assets, debt forgiveness, death duties, and taxes

Financial Account

Domestic-owned financial assets abroad (official reserve, government, private) and foreign-owned domestic financial assets

© Kaplan, Inc.

15

Additional LOS

LOS 20.f: trading blocs, common markets,
economic unions

LOS 20.j: international trade organizations

© Kaplan, Inc.

LOS 21.a Define/Distinguish
CFAI p.487, Schweser p. 231

Foreign Exchange Quotations

0.5440 GBP/USD means £0.5440 **per** USD

| Price currency |
| Base currency |

- Nominal exchange rate is the quoted rate at
  any point in time
  - Real exchange rate is the nominal exchange
    rate adjusted for inflation in each country
    compared to a base period

real exchange rate (p / b) = nominal exchange rate (p / b) $\times \left(\dfrac{CPI_{base}}{CPI_{price}} \right)$

© Kaplan, Inc.

LOS 20.i Explain
CFAI p.460, Schweser p. 223

BOP Influences

From $S - I = (G - T) + (X - M)$
$X - M = (S - I) + (T - G)$ or
= private savings – investment + government savings

- An increase (decrease) in **private or
  government savings** would improve (worsen)
  the balance of trade

  - A trade deficit due to a decrease in private or
    government savings is less desirable than
    trade deficit due to high domestic investment

© Kaplan, Inc.

Economics: Economics
in a Global Context

21. Currency Exchange Rates

KAPLAN UNIVERSITY SCHOOL OF PROFESSIONAL AND CONTINUING EDUCATION | SCHWESER

Spot Market vs. Forward Market

Spot exchange rates: Exchange rates for immediate delivery

Forward contract: An agreement to buy or sell a specific amount of a foreign currency at a future date at the quoted <u>forward exchange rate</u> (e.g., 30, 60, or 90 days in the future)

© Kaplan, Inc.   21

Market Participants

<u>Sell side</u>

Market makers: Large multinational banks

<u>Buy side</u>

- Corporations
- Investment accounts: Real money and leveraged
- Governments, sovereign wealth funds, pension plans, central banks
  - Retail market: Households (e.g., tourism)

© Kaplan, Inc.   23

Real Exchange Rate

Base period: 1/1/X1 exchange rate = 1.20 $/€

1/1/X3 exchange rate = 1.30 $/€

Base period: 1/1/X1 CPI_{USD} = 100; CPI_{euro} = 100

On 1/1/X3, CPI_{USD} = 114; CPI_{euro} = 109

Calculate the real exchange rate on 1/1/X3.

real exchange rate (p/b) = nominal exchange rate (p/b) $\times \left(\dfrac{CPI_{base}}{CPI_{price}} \right)$

= 1.30 × 109 / 114 = 1.243 $/€

The real cost of euro zone goods to a U.S. citizen has gone up by 1.243 / 1.20 − 1 = 3.6%; which is less than the nominal rate has gone up (8.3%) because U.S. inflation was higher.

© Kaplan, Inc.   20 - 3

Market Participants

Hedgers

Have an existing FX risk that they want to reduce/eliminate with forward FX contracts

Speculators

- Are not hedging an existing FX risk
- They take on FX risk with forward contracts with the expectation of earning a profit

© Kaplan, Inc.   22

Currency Appreciation or Depreciation

Consider a USD/GBP exchange rate that has gone **down** from 1.61 to 1.59.

The USD price of a British pound has gone **down** $1.59 / 1.61 - 1 = -1.24\%$, and we say the pound has **depreciated** relative to the USD by 1.24%

The GBP/USD exchange rate has gone **up** from $1 / 1.61 = 0.6211$ to $1 / 1.59 = 0.6289$.

The GBP price of a USD has gone **up** by $0.6289 / 0.6211 - 1 = 1.26\%$, and we say the USD has **appreciated** relative to the GBP by 1.26%.

© Kaplan, Inc.   24

Cross Rates Example

Given the following FX rates:

1.5600 USD/GBP and **1.4860 CHF/USD**

Calculate the CHF/GBP cross rate.

> **Just algebra:** Set up the quotes so the common currency cancels

$$\frac{USD}{GBP} \times \frac{CHF}{USD} = \frac{CHF}{GBP}$$

$$1.5600 \,\frac{USD}{GBP} \times 1.4860 \,\frac{CHF}{USD} = 2.3182 \,\frac{CHF}{GBP}$$

© Kaplan, Inc.   25 - 3

Forward Quotes—Point Basis

- Forward quote is points above (below) spot
- Point is last digit of the spot rate quote

> Last digit is 0.0001

Spot 1.4320 $/€, Forward quote + 22.1 points

Forward = $1.4320 + 22.1(0.0001) = 1.43421$ $/ €

© Kaplan, Inc.   26

Forward Quotes—Percentage Basis

Spot 1.6135 $/£

90-day forward quote is –0.29%

Forward = $1.6135 (1 - 0.0029) = \$1.6088$ $/£

We say the U.S. dollar is **trading at a forward premium** relative to the British pound.

If the forward quote is –47 points, **percentage forward quote** is $-0.0047 / 1.6135 = -0.0029 = -0.29\%$.

© Kaplan, Inc.   27

LOS 21.g Calculate/Interpret
CFAI p.511, Schweser p. 237   **Currency Exchange Rates**

Forward Discount or Premium

For FX quote of price currency / base currency

If the forward quote is **greater** than spot price:

- Base currency is trading at **forward premium**
- Price currency is trading at a **forward discount**

If the forward quote is **less** than spot price:

- Base currency is trading at **forward discount**
- Price currency is trading at a **forward premium**

© Kaplan, Inc.   28

CFA Curriculum Vol. 2,
R.21, Q.13, p. 544   **Currency Exchange Rates**

If the base currency in a forward exchange rate quote is trading at a forward discount, which of the following statements is *most* accurate?

A. The forward points will be positive.

B. The forward percentage will be negative.

C. The base currency is expected to appreciate versus the price currency.

29- 1

LOS 21.f,h Explain/Calculate/Interpret
CFAI p.513, Schweser p. 236   **Currency Exchange Rates**

No-Arbitrage Forward Exchange Rate

$$\frac{Forward(P / B)}{Spot(P / B)} = \frac{1 + Interest\ Rate_{price}}{1 + Interest\ Rate_{base}}$$

Follow the Numerator-Denominator rule: Given a quote as price/base, use interest rate of price currency in numerator and interest rate of base currency in the denominator

© Kaplan, Inc.   30

LOS 21.f,h Explain/Calculate/Interpret
CFAI p.513, Schweser p. 236   **Currency Exchange Rates**

No-Arbitrage Forward Rate

Spot rate = 1.50 \$/£; Riskless \$ interest rate is 2%; Riskless £ interest rate is 2.5%. **Calculate** the arbitrage-free, 1-year forward rate.

$$Forward(\$ / £) = \left[\frac{1 + Interest\ Rate_\$}{1 + Interest\ Rate_£} \right] \times Spot(\$ / £)$$

$$= \left[\frac{1 + 0.02}{1 + 0.025} \right] \times 1.50 = 1.4927\ \$ / £$$

U.K. interest rate is higher, so forward \$ / £ is less than spot \$ / £.

© Kaplan, Inc.   31

90-day euro Libor is 3% and 90-day AUD Libor is 4%. The spot EUR/AUD rate is 0.7276. The 90-day forward AUD/EUR no-arbitrage rate is closest to:

A. 1.3877.

B. 1.3778.

C. 1.3710.

LOS 21.j Explain
CFAI p.529, Schweser p. 240

Exchange Rates, Trade, and Capital

(X – M) = (private savings – investment) + (tax revenue – government spending) | Same as before |

(X – M) > 0, trade surplus when private savings + government surplus exceeds domestic investment

(X – M) < 0, trade deficit when private savings – domestic investment is less than budget deficit

---

LOS 21.j Explain
CFAI p.529, Schweser p. 240

Exchange Rates and Trade Deficit

Elasticities Approach

$$W_M = \frac{Imports}{Imports + Exports} \qquad W_X = \frac{Exports}{Imports + Exports}$$

ε_X and ε_M are demand elasticities of exports and imports

Classic Marshall-Lerner condition

$$\varepsilon_X + \varepsilon_M > 1$$

If the sum of export and import elasticities are greater than one, then currency depreciation will reduce trade deficit

---

LOS 21.j Explain
CFAI p.529, Schweser p. 240

Exchange Rates and Trade Deficit

J-Curve Effect

In the short run, due to existing contracts, export and import demand are relatively inelastic

➢ Currency depreciation initially leads to a larger trade deficit

In the long run, elasticities increase

➢ Currency depreciation leads to a reduction in the trade deficit

---

Currency Depreciation Effect

Sylvania's currency, S$ has depreciated relative to their trading partners' currencies. Given the following information, Sylvania's balance of trade would *most likely*:

Item	S$	Elasticity
Exports	4,000,000	0.60
Imports	6,000,000	0.75

A. worsen.
B. improve.
C. remain the same.

© Kaplan, Inc.

37 - 3

Additional Problems

KAPLAN UNIVERSITY SCHOOL OF PROFESSIONAL AND CONTINUING EDUCATION | SCHWESER

LOS 21.j Explain
CFAI p.529, Schweser p. 240

Exchange Rates and Trade Deficit

The elasticities approach only considers goods flows

The absorption approach includes the effect of currency depreciation on capital flows, as well as trade flows

© Kaplan, Inc.

36

Additional LOS

LOS 21.i: exchange rate regimes

© Kaplan, Inc.

38

CFA Curriculum Vol. 2,
R.20, Q.16, p. 480

1) The sale of mineral rights would be captured in which of the following balance of payments components?

A. Capital account.

B. Current account.

C. Financial account.

- 1

CFA Curriculum Vol. 2,
R.20, Q.19, p. 480

3) Which of the following *most likely* contributes to a current account deficit?

A. High taxes.

B. Low private savings.

C. Low private investment.

- 1

CFA Curriculum Vol. 2,
R.20, Q.17, p. 480

2) Patent fees and legal services are recorded in which of the following balance of payments components?

A. Capital account.

B. Current account.

C. Financial account.

- 1

CFA Curriculum Vol. 2,
R.21, Q.7, p. 543

4) Over the past month, the Swiss Franc (CHF) has depreciated 12 percent against pound sterling (GBP). How much has the pound sterling appreciated against the Swiss franc?

A. 12%.

B. Less than 12%.

C. More than 12%.

- 2

CFA Curriculum Vol. 2,
R.21, Q.20, p. 545

5) A large industrialized country has recently devalued its currency in an attempt to correct a persistent trade deficit. Which of the following domestic industries is *most likely* to benefit from the devaluation?

A. Luxury cars.

B. Branded prescription drugs.

C. Restaurants and live entertainment venues.

- 2

STUDY SESSION 6 ANSWERS

Reading	Slide Number	Answer
21	29	B
21	32	B
21	37	B

Additional Problems

1. A

2. B

3. B

4. C

5. A

Study Session 7

Financial Reporting and Analysis: An Introduction

Financial Reporting and Analysis

Financial Reporting and Analysis: An Introduction

22. Financial Statement Analysis: An Introduction

KAPLAN UNIVERSITY SCHOOL OF PROFESSIONAL AND CONTINUING EDUCATION | SCHWESER

Financial Reporting and Analysis

Study Session 7 Financial Reporting and Analysis: An Introduction

22. Financial Statement Analysis: An Introduction
23. Financial Reporting Mechanics
24. Financial Reporting Standards

KAPLAN UNIVERSITY SCHOOL OF PROFESSIONAL AND CONTINUING EDUCATION | SCHWESER

Financial Statement Analysis: An Introduction

LOS 22.a Describe
CFAI p. 6, Schweser p. 10

Role of Financial Statement Analysis

Using the information in a company's financial statements, along with other relevant information, to make economic decisions (e.g., evaluate securities, acquisitions, creditworthiness)

To evaluate a company's past performance and current financial position in order to form opinions about a firm's ability to earn profits and generate cash flow in the future

© Kaplan, Inc.

3

Financial Statement Analysis: An Introduction

LOS 22.a Describe
CFAI p. 6, Schweser p. 10

Role of Financial Reporting

"The objective of general purpose financial reporting is to provide financial information about the reporting entity that is useful to existing and potential investors, lenders, and other creditors in making decisions about providing resources to the entity. Those decisions involve buying, selling or holding equity and debt instruments, and providing or settling loans and other forms of credit."

IASB Conceptual Framework

© Kaplan, Inc.

2

Financial Statement Analysis:
An Introduction

LOS 22.b Describe
CFAI p. 11, Schweser p. 11

Key Financial Statements

1. **Income statement** (statement of operations or the profit and loss statement) Summarizes events over a period:

   - *Revenues* are inflows from delivering or producing goods, rendering services, or other activities that constitute the entity's ongoing major or central operations

   - *Expenses* are outflows from delivering or producing goods or services that constitute the entity's ongoing major or central operations

   - *Other income* includes gains and losses which may or may not arise in ordinary course of business

© Kaplan, Inc.

4

Financial Statement Analysis:
An Introduction

LOS 22.b Describe
CFAI p. 11, Schweser p. 11

Key Financial Statements

2. **Statement of comprehensive income** reports all changes in equity except for shareholder transactions

3. **Balance sheet**—at a point in time

   - Assets = liabilities + owners' equity

   - *Assets* are the resources controlled by the firm

   - *Liabilities* are amounts owed to lenders and other creditors

   - *Owners' equity* is the residual interest in the net assets of an entity that remains after deducting its liabilities

© Kaplan, Inc.

5

Financial Statement Analysis:
An Introduction

LOS 22.b Describe
CFAI p. 11, Schweser p. 11

Key Financial Statements

4. **Cash flow statement** reconciles beginning and ending cash balance, splitting changes into three categories:

   - *Operating cash flows (CFO)*
   - *Investing cash flows (CFI)*
   - *Financing cash flows (CFF)*

5. **Statement of changes in owners' equity**— amounts and sources of changes in shareholders' equity over the period

© Kaplan, Inc.

6

Financial Statement Analysis:
An Introduction

LOS 22.c Describe
CFAI p. 24, Schweser p. 12

Footnotes and Supplementary Schedules

- Basis of presentation
- Accounting methods and assumptions
- Further information on amounts in primary statements
- Business acquisitions/disposals
- Contingencies
- Legal proceedings
- Stock options and benefit plans
- Significant customers
- Segment data
- Quarterly data
- Related-party transactions

© Kaplan, Inc.

7

Management Discussion and Analysis

- Nature of the business
- Results from operations, business overview
- Trends in sales and expenses
- Capital resources and liquidity
- Cash flow trends
- Discussion of critical accounting choices
- Effects of inflation, price changes, and uncertainties on future results

© Kaplan, Inc.

8

Not Audited

The Audit Report

- **Audit:** *Independent review* of company's financial statements
- **Reasonable assurance** that financial statements are free of material errors
- **Audit opinion:**
  - Unqualified: "Clean" opinion
  - Qualified: Exceptions to accounting principles
  - Adverse: Statements not presented fairly
  - Disclaimer of opinion: Unable to form an opinion
- **Must provide opinion on company's internal controls under U.S. GAAP**

© Kaplan, Inc.

9

Audit Report

1. Responsibility of management to prepare accounts
   - Independence of auditors
2. Properly prepared in accordance with relevant GAAP
   - Reasonable assurance that the statements are free from material misstatement
3. Accounting principles and estimates chosen are reasonable

© Kaplan, Inc.

10

Regarding the report of independent auditors under U.S. GAAP, the audit report:

A. is unqualified if the auditors disagree with the firm on the treatment of some items.

B. must provide an opinion on the firm's internal controls.

C. does not apply to the footnotes to the financial statements.

© Kaplan, Inc.

11 - 1

Financial Reporting and Analysis

Financial Reporting and Analysis: An Introduction

23. Financial Reporting Mechanics

KAPLAN UNIVERSITY SCHOOL OF PROFESSIONAL AND CONTINUING EDUCATION | SCHWESER

Financial Statement Analysis: An Introduction

Additional LOS

LOS 22.e: information sources
LOS 22.f: financial statement analysis framework

© Kaplan, Inc.

12

Financial Reporting Mechanics

LOS 23.a Explain/Classify
CFAI p. 42, Schweser p. 19

Common Liability Accounts

- Accounts payable, trade payables
- Provisions/accrued liabilities
- Financial liabilities
- Current and deferred tax
- Unearned revenue
- Debt payable
- Bonds

© Kaplan, Inc.

15

Financial Reporting Mechanics

LOS 23.a Explain/Classify
CFAI p. 42, Schweser p. 19

Common Asset Accounts

- Cash and cash equivalents
- Accounts receivable, trade receivables
- Prepaid expenses
- Inventory
- Property, plant, and equipment (PP&E)
- Investment property
- Intangibles
- Financial assets (investment securities)
- Investments under the equity method
- Deferred tax assets

© Kaplan, Inc.

14

Common Equity Accounts

LOS 23.a Explain/Classify
CFAI p. 42, Schweser p. 19 — Financial Reporting Mechanics

- Capital at par value
- Additional paid-in capital
- Retained earnings
- Other comprehensive income
- Noncontrolling (minority) interest

© Kaplan, Inc. — 16

Common Income Statement Items

LOS 23.a Explain/Classify
CFAI p. 42, Schweser p. 19 — Financial Reporting Mechanics

- Revenue
  - Sales
  - Gains
  - Investment income
- Expense
  - Cost of goods sold
  - SG&A (selling, general, and admin)
  - Depreciation/amortization
  - Interest
  - Tax expense
  - Losses

© Kaplan, Inc. — 17

Accounting Equations

LOS 23.b Explain
CFAI p. 46, Schweser p. 20 — Financial Reporting Mechanics

Revenue − Expenses = Net income

Assets = Liabilities + Owners' equity

Assets − Liabilities = Owners' equity

Owners' equity = Contributed capital +
Retained earnings

© Kaplan, Inc. — 18

Accounting Equations

LOS 23.b Explain
CFAI p. 46, Schweser p. 20 — Financial Reporting Mechanics

	$m
Beginning retained earnings	X
Net income (loss)	X
Dividends	(X)
Ending retained earnings	X

© Kaplan, Inc. — 19

LOS 23.c Describe
CFAI p. 49, Schweser p. 21   **Financial Reporting Mechanics**

Accounting for Transactions

1. Pay a bill $E = A - L$

Asset "cash" goes down

Liability "trade payables" goes down

Equity is unchanged

2. Sell a bond (borrow money) $E = A - L$

Asset "cash" goes up by proceeds

Liability "bonds payable" goes up by proceeds

Equity is unchanged

© Kaplan, Inc.   20

LOS 23.c Describe
CFAI p. 49, Schweser p. 21   **Financial Reporting Mechanics**

Accounting for Transactions

3. Make a credit sale $E = A - L$

Asset "inventory" goes down

Asset "accounts receivable" goes up by more

Equity "retained earnings" increases by difference

On the income statement

Revenues increase, expenses increase by less

Net income and retained earnings increase

Retained earnings is an equity account

© Kaplan, Inc.   21

LOS 23.c Describe
CFAI p. 49, Schweser p. 21   **Financial Reporting Mechanics**

Accounting for Transactions

4. Buy materials on credit $E = A - L$

Asset "inventory" increases

Liability "accounts payable" increases

Equity is unchanged

5. Issue stock $E = A - L$

Asset "cash" goes up

Liabilities unchanged

Equity "common stock" increases

© Kaplan, Inc.   22

LOS 23.c Describe
CFAI p. 49, Schweser p. 21   **Financial Reporting Mechanics**

Accounting for Transactions

6. Incur an expense $E = A - L$

Liability increases

Assets unchanged

Equity "retained earnings" decreases

7. Pay a liability $E = A - L$

Asset "cash" goes down

Liability goes down

Equity unchanged

© Kaplan, Inc.   23

LOS 23.c Describe
CFAI p. 49, Schweser p. 21   **Financial Reporting Mechanics**

Accounting for Transactions

8. Declare dividend $E = A - L$

Liability "dividends payable" increases

Assets unchanged

Equity "retained earnings" decreases

9. Pay dividend $E = A - L$

Asset "cash" goes down

Liability "dividends payable" goes down

Equity unchanged

© Kaplan, Inc.   24

LOS 23.g Describe
CFAI p. 73, Schweser p. 25   **Financial Reporting Mechanics**

Statements and Security Analysis

Financial statements contain:

- Estimates   ⎱ Accruals and
- Judgements   ⎰ valuations

Analyst must review:

- MDA   ⎱ Critical accounting policies
- Footnotes   ⎰ and estimates sections

Analyst must make appropriate adjustments for analysis

© Kaplan, Inc.   25

Financial Reporting Mechanics

Which of the following would be *most likely* to change equity?

A. Collecting receivables.

B. Selling a 5-year-old machine.

C. Declaring a dividend.

© Kaplan, Inc.   26 - 2

Financial Reporting Mechanics

Additional LOS

LOS 23.d: accruals and other adjustments

LOS 23.e: relationships among statements

LOS 23.f: flow of information in an accounting
                  system

© Kaplan, Inc.   27

Financial Reporting and Analysis

Financial Reporting and Analysis: An Introduction

24. Financial Reporting Standards

KAPLAN UNIVERSITY SCHOOL OF PROFESSIONAL AND CONTINUING EDUCATION | SCHWESER

Financial Reporting Standards

LOS 24.b Describe
CFAI p. 103, Schweser p. 34

Accounting Standards

Financial Accounting Standards Board (FASB) –
U.S.

**International Accounting Standards Board
(IASB)** – many other countries

© Kaplan, Inc.

29

Financial Reporting Standards

LOS 24.b Describe
CFAI p. 103, Schweser p. 34

Financial Reporting Requirements and Regulation

Securities and Exchange Commission (SEC)

Financial Services Authority (FSA)

European Securities and Market Authority (ESMA)

**International Organization of Securities
Commissions (IOSCO)** – Goal is uniform regulation
across countries, members represent 90% of all capital
markets worldwide

© Kaplan, Inc.

30

Financial Reporting Standards

LOS 24.c Describe
CFAI p. 112, Schweser p. 35

Global Convergence of Accounting Standards

Convergence refers to reducing differences in
worldwide accounting standards

1. Increase comparability

2. Decrease problems and expenses of raising
   capital in foreign markets

3. Decrease problems and expenses of
   preparing consolidated financial statements
   for foreign subsidiaries

   Accounting standards in most major countries
   are converging over time with IFRS

© Kaplan, Inc.

31

LOS 24.c Describe
CFAI p. 112, Schweser p. 35   Financial Reporting Standards

Barriers to Standards Convergence

- **Differences in view** between standard setting bodies
- **Pressure** from business and industry groups
- Many **different countries involved**, different institutions, cultures, business environments, systems of regulation

If the application and enforcement of accounting standards differ, convergence in standards is not enough to ensure comparability of statements.

© Kaplan, Inc.

32

LOS 24.d Describe
CFAI p. 116, Schweser p. 36   Financial Reporting Standards

IFRS Conceptual Framework

Two qualitative characteristics for "decision useful" financial reporting:

1. **Relevance**

   The information can influence users' economic decisions, affect users' evaluations of past events, or forecasts of future events.

   Information should have predictive value, confirm prior expectations, or both. **Materiality** is an aspect of relevance.

© Kaplan, Inc.

33

LOS 24.d Describe
CFAI p. 116, Schweser p. 36   Financial Reporting Standards

IFRS Conceptual Framework

2. **Faithful representation**

   Information that is faithfully represented is complete, neutral (absence of bias), and free from error

   The following characteristics enhance these two primary qualitative characteristics:

   - Comparability
   - Verifiability
   - Timeliness
   - Understandability

© Kaplan, Inc.

34

LOS 24.d Describe
CFAI p. 116, Schweser p. 36   Financial Reporting Standards

Constraints

While it would be ideal to have all characteristics, in reality there are trade-offs:

- Relevance versus verifiability
- Benefits versus costs
- Excludes non-quantifiable information

© Kaplan, Inc.

35

LOS 24.g Identify
CFAI p. 129, Schweser p. 39   Financial Reporting Standards

Characteristics of a Coherent Reporting Framework

Transparency

- Accounts reflect economic substance
- Full disclosure and fair presentation

Comprehensiveness

- Full spectrum of financial transactions
- Framework flexible enough to adapt to new transactions

Consistency

- Transactions measured and presented in a similar way (across companies and time)
- Sufficient flexibility to show economic substance

© Kaplan, Inc.   36

LOS 24.g Identify
CFAI p. 129, Schweser p. 39   Financial Reporting Standards

Barriers to a Single Coherent Framework

1. Valuation
   - Historic cost: Minimal judgement—reliable
   - Fair value: Considerable judgement—relevant

2. Standard setting
   - Principles-based—few specific rules, require judgement
   - Rules-based—prescriptive but not flexible
   - Objectives-based—combines principles and rules

© Kaplan, Inc.   37

LOS 24.g Identify
CFAI p. 129, Schweser p. 39   Financial Reporting Standards

Barriers to a Single Framework

3. Measurement
   - **Asset/liability approach** results in better balance sheet information
   - **Revenue/expense approach**, focus on income statement

Standards regarding one statement will have an effect on the other—approaches may conflict.

Standard setters have favored the asset/liability approach most recently.

© Kaplan, Inc.   38

LOS 24.i Analyze
CFAI p. 134, Schweser p. 40   Financial Reporting Standards

Company Disclosures

- Critical and significant accounting policies
- Accounting estimates
- Changes in accounting policy
- Footnote disclosure and discussion in MD&A

Analyst focus:

- What policies have been discussed?
- Do the policies cover all significant transactions?
- Which balances require significant estimation?
- Have there been changes?

© Kaplan, Inc.   39

Financial Reporting and Analysis

Additional Problems

Financial Reporting Standards

Additional LOS

LOS 24.a: objective of financial statements, importance of financial reporting standards

LOS 24.e: general requirements under IFRS

LOS 24.f: IFRS and U.S. GAAP

LOS 24.h: monitoring developments in financial reporting standards

40

**CFA Curriculum Vol. 3,
R.24, Q.16, p. 142**

2) Which of the following is *not* a characteristic of a coherent financial reporting framework?

A. Timeliness.

B. Consistency.

C. Transparency.

-1

**CFA Curriculum Vol. 3,
R.24, Q.6, p. 141**

1) According to the *Conceptual Framework for Financial Reporting (2010)*, which of the following is *not* an enhancing qualitative characteristic of information in financial statements?

A. Accuracy.

B. Timeliness.

C. Comparability.

-1

CFA Curriculum Vol. 3,
R.24, Q.17, p. 142

3) Which of the following is *not* a recognized approach to standard-setting?

A. A rules-based approach.

B. An asset/liability approach.

C. A principles-based approach.

- 1

© Kaplan, Inc.

Reference Level I CFA Curriculum,
Reading 23, Problem 9

4) A company paid 20,000 on December 31, 20X1 to cover January and February rent of 8,000/mo. and a security deposit of 4,000. The *most likely* impact of this payment on reported 20X1 year-end assets is:

A. no change.

B. a decrease of 16,000.

C. a decrease of 20,000.

© Kaplan, Inc.

- 2

Additional Problems   **Financial Reporting Standards**

5) An investor would *most likely* prefer that a firm receive an audit opinion of:

A. adverse.

B. qualified.

C. unqualified.

© Kaplan, Inc.

- 1

CFA Curriculum Vol. 3,
R.22, Q.4, p. 38

6) Accounting policies, methods, and estimates used in preparing financial statements are *most likely* to be found in the:

A. auditor's report.

B. management commentary.

C. notes to the financial statements.

- 1

STUDY SESSION 7 ANSWERS

Reading	Slide Number	Answer
22	11	B
23	26	C

Additional Problems

1. A

2. A

3. B

4. A

5. C

6. C

Study Session 8

Financial Reporting and Analysis: Income Statements, Balance Sheets, and Cash Flow Statements

Income Statements, Balance Sheets, and Cash Flow Statements

25. Understanding Income Statements

KAPLAN UNIVERSITY | SCHOOL OF PROFESSIONAL AND CONTINUING EDUCATION | SCHWESER

Study Session 8

Income Statements, Balance Sheets, and Cash Flow Statements

25. Understanding Income Statements
26. Understanding Balance Sheets
27. Understanding Cash Flow Statements
28. Financial Analysis Techniques

KAPLAN UNIVERSITY | SCHOOL OF PROFESSIONAL AND CONTINUING EDUCATION | SCHWESER

© Kaplan, Inc.

LOS 25.a Describe
CFAI p. 151, Schweser p. 47   Understanding Income Statements

Income Statement

- **Revenues:** Amounts reported from the sale of goods and services in the normal course of business. Revenue less adjustments for estimated returns and allowances is known as **net revenue.**
- **Expenses:** Amounts incurred to generate revenue and include cost of goods sold, operating expenses, interest, and taxes. Expenses are grouped together by their nature.
- **Gains and losses:** Typically arise on the disposal of long-lived assets.

© Kaplan, Inc.

3

LOS 25.a Describe
CFAI p. 151, Schweser p. 47   Understanding Income Statements

Income Statement

- Alternative names:
  - Statement of operations
  - Statement of earnings
  - Profit and loss statement

  Revenue – Expenses = Net Income

- IFRS: May combine with comprehensive income items
- Two types:
  - Single step
  - Multi-step

© Kaplan, Inc.

2

Multi-step Income Statement

Revenue
- Cost of goods sold
  Gross profit
- Selling, general, and administrative expenses
  Operating profit
+ Other income and revenues
- Financing costs
+/- Unusual or infrequent items

Income before tax

> Operating or non-operating? Analyze items

© Kaplan, Inc.

4

Multi-step Income Statement

Income before tax
- Provision for income taxes   "The line"
  Income from continuing operations
+/- Income from discontinued operations   All net of tax
+/- Extraordinary items
  Net income   "The bottom line"

© Kaplan, Inc.

5

IASB Requirements for Revenue Recognition (General Principles)

1. Risk and reward of ownership transferred
2. No continuing control or management over the good sold
3. Reliable revenue measurement
4. Probable flow of economic benefits
5. Cost can be measured reliably

© Kaplan, Inc.

6

IASB Requirements for Revenue Recognition for Services

1. When the outcome can be measured reliably, revenue will be recognized by reference to the stage of completion
2. Outcome can be measured reliably if:
   - Amount of revenue can be measured
   - Probable flow of economic benefits
   - Stage of completion can be measured
   - Cost incurred and remaining cost to complete can be measured

© Kaplan, Inc.

7

SEC Requirements for Revenue Recognition

"Revenue should be recognized when it is realizable and earned" FASB

SEC additional guidance:

1. Evidence of an arrangement between buyer and seller
2. Completion of the earnings process, firm has delivered product or service
3. Price is determined
4. Assurance of payment, able to estimate probability of payment

© Kaplan, Inc.

8

Revenue Recognition Methods

Sales-basis method—used when good or service is provided at time of sale, cash, or credit with high payment probability (majority of transactions)

Exceptions (construction contracts)

1. **Percentage-of-completion method**—used for L-T projects under contract, with **reliable estimates** of revenues, costs, and completion time

© Kaplan, Inc.

9

Revenue Recognition Methods

2. **Completed-contract method (U.S. GAAP)**—used for L-T projects with no contract, or unreliable estimates of revenue or costs; revenue and expenses are not recognized until **project is completed**
   (IFRS: Report revenue but no profit)

For both U.S. GAAP and IFRS, if a loss is expected under either the percentage-of-completion or completed-contract method, it must be recognized in the period in which a loss on the overall project becomes expected.

© Kaplan, Inc.

10

Revenue Recognition Methods

Installment Sale: Payments for an asset purchase are made over an extended period

Under IFRS

- Sale price is recorded as revenue at the time of sale, interest is recognized as revenue over the life of the contract
  - Exception: Some real estate sales require deferral of revenue recognition
    - If outcome cannot be reliably estimated, revenue recognition under IFRS is similar to cost recovery method (however, the term is not used)

© Kaplan, Inc.

11

Revenue Recognition Methods

Under U.S. GAAP

3. Installment method used when firm cannot estimate likelihood of collection on an installment sale, but cost of goods/services is known; revenue and profit are based on percentage of cash collected.

4. Cost recovery method (most extreme)—used when cost of goods/services is unknown and firm cannot estimate the likelihood of collection; only recognize profit after all costs are recovered

Use of these methods is rare, especially for sale of anything but real estate.

© Kaplan, Inc.

12

Percentage-of-Completion Method

Cumulative revenue

$$\frac{\text{Total costs to date}}{\text{Total project cost}} \times \text{Sales price} = \quad X$$

Revenue recognized in prior years	(X)
This period's revenue	X
Costs incurred in period	(X)
Profit recognized in period	X

Must do this calculation if total cost estimate changes

© Kaplan, Inc.

13

Percentage-of-Completion Method

Wildon Properties Ltd. has a contract to build a hotel for $2,000,000 to be received in equal installments over 4 years.

A reliable estimate of total cost of this contract is $1,600,000.

During the first year, Ledesma incurred $400,000 in cost. During the second year, $500,000 of costs were incurred and the estimate of total cost did not change.

Calculate the revenue and profit to be recognized in each of the first two years.

© Kaplan, Inc.

14

Percentage-of-Completion Method
Solution

Year 1: $2,000,000 × (400,000 / 1,600,000)

Revenue = $500,000

Profit = $500,000 − $400,000 = $100,000

Year 2: $2,000,000 × (900,000 / 1,600,000)
− $500,000

Revenue = $625,000

Profit = $625,000 − $500,000 = $125,000

© Kaplan, Inc.

15 - 6

Completed-Contract Method

Revenue and expenses are not recognized until **project is completed**

Example: Building a hotel for $40 million, cost to build is $32 million; cost incurred in Year 1 is $6.4 million

revenue = 0; expense = 0; income = 0

On completion/final year:

revenue = $40m; expenses = $32m; income = $8m

© Kaplan, Inc.

16

IFRS: Long-term Contracts With Uncertain Outcome

Revenue and expenses are recognized over the project's life; however, no profit is recorded until **project is completed** (similar to completed-contract)

Example: Building a hotel for €40 million, cost to build is €32 million; cost incurred in Year 1 is €6.4 million

Revenue = 6.4m; expense = 6.4m; income = 0

On completion/final year:

Income = €8m

© Kaplan, Inc.

17

Cost Recovery Method – Example

During 20X0, Cook, Inc. sold $20,000 of services, but the cost of providing this service was unclear at the outset of the contract. During 20X0 and 20X1, Cook collected $8,000 and $12,000, respectively, of its receivables. The project was completed during 20X1, at which time the company had incurred total costs of $10,000.

Under the cost recovery method, what are the sales and gross profit to be reported in each of the two years?

© Kaplan, Inc.

18

Cost Recovery Method – Solution

	20X0	20X1
Sales	8,000	12,000
Cost of sales	(8,000)	(2,000)
Gross profit	0	10,000

© Kaplan, Inc.

19 - 3

Barter

- Exchange of goods or services between two parties (no exchange of cash)
- A agrees to exchange inventory for a service provided by B
- **IFRS:** Revenue = fair value of similar non-barter transactions with unrelated parties
- **U.S. GAAP:** Revenue = fair value only if the company has received cash payments for such services historically (otherwise record sale at carrying value of asset)

© Kaplan, Inc.   20

Gross vs. Net Reporting

- Internet-based merchandising companies
- Sell product but never hold in inventory
- Arrangement for supplier to ship directly to end customer

	Gross Reporting	Sales commission
Revenue	$ 100	$
Cost of good sold	80	
Gross profit	20	Net sale 20

© Kaplan, Inc.   21

Gross vs. Net Reporting

- **U.S. GAAP:** Report gross if company:
  - Is primary obligator
  - Bears inventory risk
  - Bears credit risk
  - Can choose supplier
  - Has latitude to set price

If criteria are not met, then company is acting as an agent: report net

© Kaplan, Inc.   22

Implications for Analysis

Review revenue recognition policies in footnotes:

- Earlier revenue recognition—aggressive
- Later revenue recognition—conservative
- Consider estimates used in methods
- Assess how different policies would affect financial ratios

© Kaplan, Inc.   23

Understanding Income Statements

Project cost estimate = $10 million; contract totals $12 million; $2 million of costs occur in Years 1 and 2; invoiced amounts $4 million in Year 1 and $3 million in Year 2; $1 million in cash collected each year. Year 2 income under percentage of completion is:

A. $1 million.

B. $400,000.

C. $1 million loss.

© Kaplan, Inc.

24 - 2

LOS 25.d Describe
CFAI p. 168, Schweser p. 55   Understanding Income Statements

Expense Recognition

- Accrual basis—matching principle
  - Match costs against associated revenues
  - Examples
    - Inventory
    - Depreciation/amortization
    - Warranty expense
    - Doubtful debt expense
- Period expenses
  - Expenditures that less directly match the timing of revenues (e.g., admin costs)

© Kaplan, Inc.

25

LOS 25.d Describe
CFAI p. 168, Schweser p. 55   Understanding Income Statements

Analysis Implications

- Inventory valuation
- Warranty expense
- Depreciation
- Amortization
- Doubtful debt provisions
- Revenue recognition

} All require significant estimates and assumptions affecting net income

- Review year-on-year consistency
- Review footnotes and MD&A

© Kaplan, Inc.

26

LOS 25.d Describe
CFAI p. 168, Schweser p. 55   Understanding Income Statements

Amortization

- Amortization of intangible assets (e.g., patents)
- Spreading cost over life
- If the earnings pattern cannot be established, use straight line (IAS 38)
- IFRS and U.S. GAAP firms both typically amortize straight-line with no residual value
- Goodwill not amortized—checked annually for impairment

© Kaplan, Inc.

27

Unusual or Infrequent Items

- "Or" is the key word that describes these items
- Reported pretax before net income from continuing operations (above the line)
- Items include:
  - Gain (loss) from disposal of a *business segment or assets*
  - Gain (loss) from sale of investment in subsidiary
  - Provisions for environmental remediation
  - Impairments, write-offs, write-downs, restructuring
  - Integration expense for recently acquired business

© Kaplan, Inc.   28

Discontinued Operations

- Operations that management has decided to dispose of but (1) has not done so yet or (2) did so in current year after it generated profit or loss
- Reported net of taxes after net income from continuing operations (below the line)
- Assets, operations, and financing activities must be physically and operationally distinct from firm

© Kaplan, Inc.   29

Extraordinary Items (U.S. GAAP)

- Items that are both unusual and infrequent
- Reported net of taxes after net income from continuing operations (below the line)

Items include:

- Losses from expropriation of assets
- Gains or losses from early retirement of debt (when judged to be both unusual and infrequent)
- Uninsured losses from natural disaster
- Prohibited under IFRS

© Kaplan, Inc.   30

Accounting Changes

Two types of accounting changes:

1. Change in accounting principle (e.g., inventory cost method)

   Retrospective application: IFRS and U.S. GAAP require prior years' data shown in the financial statements to be adjusted

© Kaplan, Inc.   31

LOS 25.e Describe
CFAI p. 178, Schweser p. 61   Understanding Income Statements

Accounting Changes

2. Change in accounting estimate (e.g., change in depreciation method or useful life, salvage value)

   - Does not require restatement of prior period earnings
   - Disclosed in footnotes
   - Typically, changes do not affect cash flow

LOS 25.e Describe
CFAI p. 178, Schweser p. 61   Understanding Income Statements

Accounting Changes

Prior period adjustments

- Correcting errors or changing from an incorrect accounting method to one that is acceptable under GAAP
- Typically requires restatement of prior period financial statements
- Must **disclose** the nature of the error and its effect on net income

LOS 25.f Distinguish
CFAI p. 183, Schweser p. 63   Understanding Income Statements

Non-Operating Items

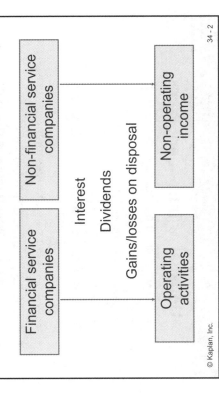

LOS 25.g,h Describe/Calculate/Interpret/Distinguish
CFAI p. 184, Schweser p. 63   Understanding Income Statements

Simple vs. Complex Capital Structures

- A simple capital structure contains no *potentially* dilutive securities
  - Firm reports only basic EPS
- A complex capital structure contains *potentially* dilutive securities
  - Firm must report both basic and diluted EPS

LOS 25.g,h Describe/Calculate/Interpret/Distinguish
CFAI p. 184, Schweser p. 63   Understanding Income Statements

Dilutive vs. Antidilutive Securities

Potentially dilutive securities:

- Stock options
- Warrants
- Convertible debt
- Convertible preferred stock
- Dilutive securities decrease EPS if exercised or converted to common stock
- Antidilutive securities increase EPS if exercised or converted to common stock

© Kaplan, Inc.

36

LOS 25.g,h Describe/Calculate/Interpret/Distinguish
CFAI p. 184, Schweser p. 63   Understanding Income Statements

Calculating Basic EPS

$$\text{Basic EPS} = \frac{\text{Net income} - \text{preferred dividends}}{\text{Weighted average \# common stock}}$$

- Net income minus preferred dividends equals earnings available to common stockholders
- Note that common stock dividends are not subtracted from net income

© Kaplan, Inc.

37

LOS 25.g,h Describe/Calculate/Interpret/Distinguish
CFAI p. 184, Schweser p. 63   Understanding Income Statements

Stock Dividends and Stock Splits

- A 10% stock dividend increases shares outstanding by 10%
- A 2-for-1 stock split increases shares outstanding by 100%
- In calculating the weighted average shares outstanding, stock dividends and splits are applied retroactively to the beginning of the year, or the stock's issue date for new stock
- Although weighted average shares are actually based on days, the exam is likely to use months

© Kaplan, Inc.

38

LOS 25.g,h Describe/Calculate/Interpret/Distinguish
CFAI p. 184, Schweser p. 63   Understanding Income Statements

Calculating the Weighted-Average Number of Shares Outstanding

1/1/X3	Shares outstanding	10,000
4/1/X3	Shares issued	4,000
7/1/X3	10% stock dividend	
9/1/X3	Shares repurchased	3,000

Shares adjusted for the 10% dividend:		
1/1/X3	Initial shares (× 1.1)	**11,000**
4/1/X3	Shared issued (× 1.1)	**4,400**
9/1/X3	Shares repurchased (no adj.)	**3,000**

© Kaplan, Inc.

39 - 3

Calculating the Weighted-Average Number of Shares Outstanding

Initial shares (11,000) (12 months)	132,000
Shares issued (4,400) (9 months)	39,600
Shares repurchased (3,000) (4 months)	(12,000)
Total weighted shares	159,600
Weighted average shares outstanding 159,600 / 12	13,300

© Kaplan, Inc.

40 - 5

Diluted Earnings Per Share

$$\left(\frac{net\ income - preferred\ dividends}{weighted\ average\ shares} + \frac{shares\ from\ conversion\ of\ conv.\ pfd.\ shares} {} + \frac{convertible\ preferred\ dividend} {shares\ from\ conversion\ of\ conv.\ debt} + \frac{convertible\ debt\ interest(1-t)} {shares\ issuable\ from\ options/warrants}\right)$$

Include only if security is dilutive

Include only if security is dilutive

© Kaplan, Inc.

41

Checking for Dilution

- Only those securities that **would reduce EPS** below basic EPS if converted are used in the calculation of diluted EPS

<u>Conv. pfd</u>: is dividends/new shares < basic?

<u>Conv. debt</u>: is interest (1 – t) / new shares < basic?

<u>Options and warrants</u>: is avg. price > ex. price?

If answer is **yes**, the security is **dilutive**

© Kaplan, Inc.

42

Convertible Preferred Stock – Example

Earnings available to common, year to 12/31/X1	$4,000,000
Common stock	2,000,000 sh.
Basic EPS	$2.00

$5,000,000 of 7% convertible preferred stock is outstanding all year. The terms of conversion are that every $10 nominal value of preferred stock can be converted to 1.1 common shares.

Calculate fully diluted EPS for 20X1.

© Kaplan, Inc.

43

Convertible Preferred Stock – Example

	$
Earnings available to common	4,000,000
Add: Preferred dividend saved	350,000
	4,350,000

No. of common stock shares if preferred shares were converted:

Outstanding all year	2,000,000
On conversion $5,000,000 / 10 × 1.1	550,000
	2,550,000

© Kaplan, Inc.

44 - 2

Convertible Preferred Stock – Example

Check for dilution:

$$\frac{\text{Preferred Dividend}}{\text{Shares Created}} \quad < \quad \text{Basic EPS?}$$

$$\frac{\$350,000}{550,000} \quad < \quad \$2.00$$

Diluted EPS:

$$\frac{\$4,350,000}{2,550,000} = \$1.71$$

© Kaplan, Inc.

45 - 2

Convertible Bonds – Example

Earnings available to common, year to 12/31/X1	$2,500,000
Common stock	1,000,000 sh.
Basic EPS	$2.50
Tax rate	30%

$2,000,000 par value of 5% convertible bonds have been outstanding all year. Each $1,000 par value convertible bond can be converted to 120 common shares.

Calculate fully diluted EPS for 20X1.

© Kaplan, Inc.

46

Convertible Bonds – Example

	$	$
Earnings available to common		2,500,000
Add: Interest saved	100,000	
Less: Tax @ 30%	(30,000)	
		70,000
		2,570,000

No. of common shares if bonds were converted:

Outstanding	1,000,000
On conversion $2,000,000 / $1,000 × 120	240,000
	1,240,000

© Kaplan, Inc.

47 - 3

Dilutive Stock Options –
Treasury Stock Method

Dilutive only when the exercise price is less than the average market price

STEPS

1. Calculate number of common shares created if options are exercised

2. Calculate cash received from exercise

3. Calculate number of shares that can be purchased at the average market price with exercise proceeds

4. Calculate net increase in common shares outstanding

© Kaplan, Inc.   49

Dilutive Stock Options – Example

Step 1 – Assume all options are exercised

Shares issued = 100,000

Step 2 – Calculate Cash Proceeds

Proceeds if all options exercised: 100,000 × $15 = $1,500,000

Step 3 – Calculate number of shares that can be bought at average price

$$\frac{\$1,500,000}{\$20} = 75,000 \text{ shares}$$

Step 4 – Calculate Net Increase In Common Stock

Total shares needed	100,000
Shares "purchased" with proceeds	75,000
Number of new shares needed	25,000

© Kaplan, Inc.   51 - 4

Convertible Bonds – Solution

Check for dilution:

Interest savings $(1-t)$ <   Basic EPS?

Shares created

$$\frac{\$70,000}{240,000} \quad < \quad \$2.50$$

Diluted EPS:

$$\frac{\$2,570,000}{1,240,000} = \$2.07$$

© Kaplan, Inc.   48 - 2

Dilutive Employee Stock Options— Example

Earnings for equity in year to 31/Dec/X1	$1,200,000
Weighted average no. of common stock shares	500,000
Average price of common stock during year	$20
Exercise price	$15
Number of options outstanding in the year	100,000
Basic EPS	**$2.40**

Calculate diluted EPS for 20X1.

© Kaplan, Inc.   50

Dilutive Stock Options

Diluted EPS: $\dfrac{\$1,200,000}{525,000} = \$2.29$

© Kaplan, Inc.

52 - 1

Vertical Common-Size Income Statements

Income statement account   *e.g.,* $\dfrac{Marketing\ expense}{Sales}$

$\dfrac{}{Sales}$

- Converts income statement to relative percentages
- Useful for comparing entities of differing sizes
- Compare % to strategy in MD&A
- Time series or cross-section use
- Gross and net profit margin are common-size ratios

© Kaplan, Inc.

53

Comprehensive Income

Comprehensive income =
Net income + Other comprehensive income

Net income from income statement	X
Δ Foreign currency translation adjustment	X/(X)
Δ Minimum pension liability adjustment	X/(X)
Δ Unrealized gains or losses on derivatives contracts accounted for as hedges	X/(X)
Δ Unrealized gains and losses on available for sale securities	X/(X)
Comprehensive income	X

Other Comprehensive Income

© Kaplan, Inc.

54

Jan 1   10,000 shares
Mar 1   3,000 shares issued
July 1   20% stock dividend
Nov 1   3,000 shares repurchased

The weighted average number of shares outstanding over the year equals:

A. 12,000.
B. 11,300.
C. 14,500.

© Kaplan, Inc.

55 - 2

Financial Reporting and Analysis

Income Statements, Balance Sheets, and Cash Flow Statements

26. Understanding Balance Sheets

KAPLAN UNIVERSITY SCHOOL OF PROFESSIONAL AND CONTINUING EDUCATION | SCHWESER

LOS 26.a Describe
CFAI p. 212, Schweser p. 86 — Understanding Balance Sheet

Components and Format of Balance Sheet

Balance Sheet	$m		$m
Current assets		Current liabilities	70
Cash	50	Long-term liabilities	180
Others	100		250
	150	Owners' equity	
Long-lived assets		Contributed capital	100
Investments	20	Retained earnings	70
PP&E	200		170
Intangibles	50	Liabilities and equity	420
Total assets	420		

© Kaplan, Inc.

57

LOS 26.a Describe
CFAI p. 212, Schweser p. 86 — Understanding Balance Sheets

Assets

Asset recognition:
- Probable future flow of future economic benefit to the entity
- Measurable with reliability

Assets Disclosed on the B/S

Cash and equivalents
Inventories
Trade and other receivables
Prepaid expenses
Financial assets
Deferred tax assets

Property, plant, and equipment
Investment property
Intangible assets
Equity a/c investments
Natural resources
Assets held for sale

© Kaplan, Inc.

58

LOS 26.a Describe
CFAI p. 212, Schweser p. 86 — Understanding Balance Sheets

Liabilities

Liability recognition:
- Probable sacrifice of future economic benefit to the entity as a result of past transactions/events
- Amounts received but not reported as revenue in the income statement (deferred/unearned revenue)
- Amounts reported as expenses but which have not been paid

Liabilities Disclosed on the B/S

Bank borrowings
Notes payable
Provisions
Unearned revenues

Accounts payable
Financial liabilities
Accrued liabilities
Deferred tax liabilities

© Kaplan, Inc.

59

LOS 26.a Describe
CFAI p. 212, Schweser p. 86

Equity

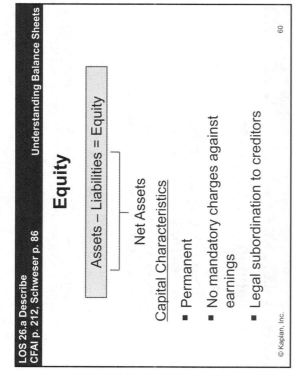

Assets – Liabilities = Equity

Net Assets

Capital Characteristics

- Permanent
- No mandatory charges against earnings
- Legal subordination to creditors

© Kaplan, Inc.   60

LOS 26.b Describe
CFAI p. 212, Schweser p. 87

Balance Sheet Analysis

Uses of balance sheet analysis

- Assessing liquidity, solvency, and ability to make distributions to shareholders

Limitations

- Mixed measurement conventions:
  - Historic cost
  - Amortized cost
  - Fair value
- Fair values may change after balance sheet date
- Off-balance-sheet assets and liabilities

© Kaplan, Inc.   61

LOS 26.c Describe
CFAI p. 215, Schweser p. 87

Balance Sheet Format

- Report format
  - Assets, liabilities, and equity in a single column
- Account format
  - Assets on the left
  - Liabilities and equity on the right
- Classified balance sheet
  - Grouping of accounts into sub-categories:
    - Current vs. non-current
    - Financial vs. non-financial
    - Liquidity-based presentation (financial institutions)

© Kaplan, Inc.   62

LOS 26.d,e Distinguish/Describe
CFAI p. 215, Schweser p. 87

Current Assets

- **Current assets** include cash and other assets that will likely be converted into cash or used up within one year or one operating cycle, whichever is greater
- The **operating cycle** is the time it takes to produce or purchase inventory, sell the product, and collect the cash
- Current assets presented in the order of liquidity
- Current assets reveal information about the operating activities/capacity of the firm

© Kaplan, Inc.   63

Current Assets

- Cash and cash equivalents: amortized cost or fair value
- Marketable securities: amortized cost or fair value
- Accounts receivable/trade receivables: net realizable value
- Inventories:
  - Raw materials, work in process, finished goods
  - Manufacturing (standardized costs)
    - Cost flow methodology (FIFO, Avco, LIFO)
- Prepaid expenses: historic cost
- Deferred tax assets: net of valuation allowance

© Kaplan, Inc.   64

Noncurrent Assets

- Assets held for continuing use within the business, not resale
- Assets not consumed or disposed of in the current period
- Represent the infrastructure from which the entity operates
- Provides information on the firm's investing activities

© Kaplan, Inc.   65

Accounting for Long-Term Assets

Long-term assets convey benefits over time

- Tangible assets (e.g., land, buildings, equipment, natural resources)
- Intangible assets (e.g., copyrights, patents, trademarks, franchises, and goodwill)
- Investment property (IFRS only)—generates investment income or capital appreciation

Plant, property, and equipment recorded at purchase cost including shipping and installation, or construction cost including labor, materials, overhead, and interest

© Kaplan, Inc.   66

Goodwill

Goodwill is the difference between acquisition price and the fair market value of the acquired firm's net assets

The additional amount paid represents the amount paid for assets not recorded on the balance sheet

	$	Fair value
Acquisition price	X	involves
FMV net assets acquired	(X)	management discretion—
Goodwill	X	goodwill is not amortized!

© Kaplan, Inc.   67

LOS 26.d,e Distinguish/Describe
CFAI p. 215, Schweser p. 87   Understanding Balance Sheets

Goodwill Analysis

- Impairment indicates that goodwill often results from overpayment to acquire entity
- Remove the impact of goodwill from ratios
  - Remove goodwill from assets
  - Remove any impairment from income statement
  - Evaluate business acquisitions considering:
    - Purchase price
    - Net assets
    - Earnings prospects

© Kaplan, Inc.   68

LOS 26.d,e Distinguish/Describe
CFAI p. 215, Schweser p. 87   Understanding Balance Sheets

Financial Assets/Liabilities

- Stocks
- Bonds
- Receivables
- Notes receivable
- Notes payable
- Loans
- Derivatives

© Kaplan, Inc.   69

LOS 26.d,e Distinguish/Describe
CFAI p. 215, Schweser p. 87   Understanding Balance Sheets

Fair Value Assets and Liabilities

Financial assets
- Trading securities
- Available-for-sale securities
- Derivatives (standalone or embedded in a non-derivative instrument)
- Assets with fair value exposures hedged by derivatives

Financial liabilities
- Derivatives
- Non-derivative investments with fair value exposures hedged by derivatives

© Kaplan, Inc.   70

LOS 26.d,e Distinguish/Describe
CFAI p. 215, Schweser p. 87   Understanding Balance Sheets

Cost or Amortized Cost

Financial assets
- Unlisted instruments
- Held-to-maturity investments
- Loans
- Receivables

Financial liabilities
- All other liabilities (e.g., bonds, notes payable, etc.)

© Kaplan, Inc.   71

Marketable Securities

Classification of securities based on company's intent with regard to eventual sale:

Held-to-maturity securities
- Debt securities which the company intends to hold to maturity
- Securities are carried at cost
- I/S income and realized gains/(losses) on disposal

Available-for-sale securities
- May be sold to satisfy company needs
- Debt or equity
- Current or non-current
- Carried on balance sheet at market value
- Income statement same as HTM method

© Kaplan, Inc.

72

Marketable Securities

Trading securities
- Acquired for the purpose of selling in the near term
- Carried on the balance sheet as current assets at market value
- Income statement includes dividends, realized and unrealized gains/losses

© Kaplan, Inc.

73

Marketable Securities Example

Ellerslie, Inc. purchased 30 5% annual-pay, $1,000 face value bonds on January 1, 20x4 at par. The market price of the bonds on December 31, 20x4 was $1,010.

Interest on the bonds of $30 \times 0.05 \times \$1,000 = \$1,500$ was paid during the year.

What are the balance sheet and income statement entries for 20x4 if these bonds are classified by the firm as held-to-maturity, available-for-sale, or trading securities?

© Kaplan, Inc.

74

Marketable Securities Example

Treatment of interest received

- The interest received, $1,500, will **be reported as income** on the income statement for 20x4, regardless of how the securities are classified by the firm

© Kaplan, Inc.

75

Marketable Securities Example

Treatment of unrealized gains

- The 30 × ($1,010 – $1,000) = $300 in unrealized gains are treated as follows:
  - **Trading securities**
    - $300 in gains reported on 20x4 income statement, which increases net income and retained earnings
    - The 20x4 balance sheet will reflect the increase in the bonds' value: assets increase, equity increases from increase in retained earnings

© Kaplan, Inc.

76

Marketable Securities Example

Treatment of unrealized gains

- **Available-for-sale securities**
  - $300 unrealized gains reported as other comprehensive income for 20x4, not reported on income statement
  - The 20x4 balance sheet will reflect the increase in the bonds' value: assets increase and equity increases from increase in other comprehensive income

© Kaplan, Inc.

77

Marketable Securities Example

Treatment of unrealized gains

- **Held-to-maturity securities**
  - Unrealized gains are not reported on the income statement or as other comprehensive income
  - The balance sheet will show the bonds at amortized cost; unrealized gains do not affect assets or equity
  - Note that equity securities cannot be classified as held-to-maturity, as they have no maturity dates

© Kaplan, Inc.

78

Marketable Securities

Type of Security	Held to maturity	Available for sale	Trading
Interest income	Income statement	Income statement	Income statement
Unrealized G/L	Carried at cost	OCI to BS	Income statement
Realized G/L	Income statement	Income statement	Income statement

© Kaplan, Inc.

79

LOS 26.d,e Distinguish/Describe
CFAI p. 215, Schweser p. 87   Understanding Balance Sheets

Current Liabilities

Satisfies any of the following four criteria:

1. Expected to be settled in the entity's normal operating cycle

2. Held primarily for the purpose of being traded

3. Is due to be settled < 12 months from the balance sheet date

4. The entity does not have a right to defer settlement for > 12 months

All other liabilities—noncurrent

© Kaplan, Inc.

80

LOS 26.d,e Distinguish/Describe
CFAI p. 215, Schweser p. 87   Understanding Balance Sheets

Current Liabilities

- Accounts payable/trade payables
- Notes payable
- Current portion of long-term debt
- Accrued liabilities
- Taxes payable
- Unearned revenue

© Kaplan, Inc.

81

LOS 26.f Describe
CFAI p. 241, Schweser p. 96   Understanding Balance Sheets

Components of Equity

- Capital contributed by owners
  - Issued and authorized
- Preferred stock (irredeemable)
- Treasury stock (reduces equity)
- Retained earnings
- Noncontrolling (minority) interest
- Accumulated other comprehensive income

© Kaplan, Inc.

82

LOS 26.f Describe
CFAI p. 241, Schweser p. 96   Understanding Balance Sheets

Statement of Changes in Stockholders' Equity

	Common Stock	Retained Earnings (in thousands)	Accumulated Other Comprehensive Income (loss)	Total
Beginning balance	$49,234	$26,664	($406)	$75,492
Net income		6,994		6,994
Net unrealized loss on available-for-sale securities			(40)	(40)
Net unrealized loss on cash flow hedges			(56)	(56)
Adjustments to net pension liability			(26)	(26)
Cumulative translation adjustment			42	42
Comprehensive income				6,914
Issuance of common stock	1,282			1,282
Repurchases of common stock	(6,200)			(6,200)
Dividends		(2,360)		(2,360)
Ending balance	$44,316	$31,298	($486)	$75,128

OCI

© Kaplan, Inc.

83

Common Size Balance Sheet

$$\frac{\text{Balance sheet account}}{\text{Total assets}} \quad e.g., \quad \frac{\text{Inventory}}{\text{Total assets}}$$

Uses:

Comparisons over time (trend analysis)

Cross-sectional comparisons

© Kaplan, Inc.   84

Liquidity Ratios

Current ratio $\dfrac{\text{Current assets}}{\text{Current liabilities}}$

Quick ratio $\dfrac{\text{Current assets} - \text{inventory}}{\text{Current liabilities}}$

Cash ratio $\dfrac{\text{Cash} + \text{marketable securities}}{\text{Current liabilities}}$

© Kaplan, Inc.   85

Solvency Ratios

Long-term debt to equity $\dfrac{\text{Total long-term debt}}{\text{Total equity}}$

Debt to equity $\dfrac{\text{Total debt}}{\text{Total equity}}$

Total debt $\dfrac{\text{Total debt}}{\text{Total assets}}$

Financial leverage $\dfrac{\text{Total assets}}{\text{Total equity}}$

© Kaplan, Inc.   86

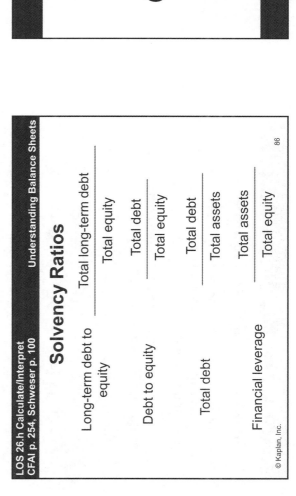

Income Statements, Balance Sheets, and Cash Flow Statements

27. Understanding Cash Flow Statements

KAPLAN UNIVERSITY   SCHOOL OF PROFESSIONAL AND CONTINUING EDUCATION | SCHWESER

Importance of Cash Flow Statement

Net income from accrual accounting does not tell us about the **sources and uses of cash** to meet liabilities and operating needs

The statement of cash flows has **three components** under both IFRS and U.S. GAAP:

- Cash provided or used by **operating** activities
- Cash provided or used by **investing** activities
- Cash provided or used in **financing** activities

© Kaplan, Inc.

88

Operating Cash Flows (CFO)

	$
Cash received from customers	X
Cash dividends received	X
Cash interest received	X
Other cash income	X
Payments to suppliers	(X)
Cash expenses (wages, etc.)	(X)
Cash interest paid	(X)
Cash taxes paid	(X)
CFO	X/(X)

© Kaplan, Inc.

89

Investing Cash Flows (CFI)

- Purchases of property, plant, and equipment
- Proceeds from sales of assets
- Investments in joint ventures and affiliates
- Payments for businesses acquired
- Purchases and sales of intangibles
- Purchases or sales of marketable securities

Excludes:

- Trading securities (part of CFO)
- Cash equivalents (part of balance sheet cash)

© Kaplan, Inc.

90

Financing Cash Flows

- Issue and redemption of:
  - Common stock
  - Preferred stock
  - Treasury stock repurchases
  - Debt
  - Dividend payments (dividends rec'd CFO— U.S. GAAP)
- Excludes:
  - Indirect financing via accounts payable (CFO)

© Kaplan, Inc.

91

LOS 27.b Describe
CFAI p. 269, Schweser p. 111
Understanding Cash Flow
Statements

Non-Cash Investing and Financing Activities

- Several types of transactions do not involve the payment or receipt of cash and are not reflected in financing and investing cash flows, but are <u>disclosed</u> <u>in the footnotes or other schedules</u>

Non-cash financing and investing activities:

- Converting debt or preferred into common equity
- Assets acquired under capital leases
- Purchase of assets via issuance of debt/equity
- Exchanging one non-cash asset for another
- Stock dividends

© Kaplan, Inc.   92

LOS 27.c Contrast
CFAI p. 269, Schweser p. 111
Understanding Cash Flow
Statements

U.S. GAAP vs. IFRS

	U.S. GAAP	IFRS
Interest received	CFO	CFO or CFI
Interest paid	CFO	CFO or CFF
Dividends received	CFO	CFO or CFI
Dividends paid	CFF	CFO or CFF
Taxes paid	CFO	CFO or CFI & CFF
Bank overdraft	CFF	*

* Considered part of cash and cash equivalents

© Kaplan, Inc.   93

LOS 27.d Distinguish/Describe
CFAI p. 270, Schweser p. 112
Understanding Cash Flow
Statements

Statement of Cash Flow: Direct vs. Indirect Method

Direct vs. indirect method refers only to the calculation of CFO; the value of CFO is the same for both methods; CFI and CFF are unaffected

- <u>Direct method</u>: Identify actual cash inflows and outflows (e.g., collections from customers, amounts paid to suppliers)

- <u>Indirect method</u>: Begin with net income and make necessary adjustments to get operating cash flow

© Kaplan, Inc.   94

LOS 27.e Describe
CFAI p. 280, Schweser p. 114
Understanding Cash Flow
Statements

Linkages Between Statements

Last year's
balance sheet   Accounts Receivable 'T' Account

Amount B/Fwd	18,000		
		198,000	Cash collections
Sales	200,000		
		20,000	Amount C/Fwd
	218,000	218,000	

This year's
income statement

This year's
balance sheet

© Kaplan, Inc.   95 - 5

Cash Inflows and Outflows

General rules regarding increases and
decreases in balance sheet items over time:

	Increase	Decrease
Assets	outflow	inflow
Liabilities & Equity	inflow	outflow

e.g.: An increase in AR or inventory uses cash

An increase in payables generates cash

Adjust net income for these changes
(indirect)

© Kaplan, Inc.

96

Ecclestone Industries—Example

Ecclestone Industries has the following income
statement for 20X8 and balance sheets for 20X8 and
20X9. You are to construct the statement of cash flows
using the **indirect method**.

Additional information:
Equipment was purchased for $50,000

© Kaplan, Inc.

97

Income Statement for Year to 31 December 20X9

		$
Sales revenue		200,000
Expenses:		
Cost of goods sold	80,000	
Salaries	10,000	
Depreciation	14,000	
Interest	1,000	
		105,000
		95,000
Gain from sale of PPE		20,000
Pre-tax income		115,000
Provision for taxes		40,000
Net income		75,000

© Kaplan, Inc.

98

Ecclestone Balance Sheet Data

Balance Sheets	20X8 $	20X9 $
Current assets		
Cash	18,000	66,000
Accounts receivable	18,000	20,000
Inventory	14,000	10,000
Non-current assets		
Gross PPE	282,000	312,000
Accum. Depr.	(80,000)	(84,000)
Total Assets	**252,000**	**324,000**

© Kaplan, Inc.

99

Slide 100

Balance Sheets

	20X8 $	20X9 $
Current liabilities		
Accounts payable	10,000	18,000
Salaries payable	16,000	9,000
Interest payable	6,000	7,000
Taxes payable	8,000	10,000
Dividends payable	2,000	12,000
Noncurrent liabilities		
Bonds	20,000	30,000
Deferred taxes	30,000	40,000
Stockholders' equity		
Common stock	100,000	80,000
Retained earnings	60,000	118,000
Total Liabilities & Equity	**252,000**	**324,000**

© Kaplan, Inc.

100

Slide 101

Indirect Method CFO

Steps

1. Start with net income
2. Adjust net income for changes in relevant balance sheet items:

> Increases in an asset: deduct
> Increase in a liability: add
> Decrease in an asset: add
> Decrease in a liability: deduct

© Kaplan, Inc.

101

Slide 102

Indirect Method (continued)

3. Eliminate depreciation and amortization by adding them back (they've been deducted in arriving at net income but are non-cash expenses)

4. Eliminate gains on disposal by deducting them and losses on disposal by adding them back (these are CFI, not CFO)

© Kaplan, Inc.

102

Slide 103

Indirect Method Solution

	$
Net income	75,000
Add: Depreciation	14,000
Less: Gain from sale of PPE	(20,000)
Add: Increase in deferred taxes	10,000
Current asset adjustments	
Less: Increase in accounts receivable	(2,000)
Add: Decrease in inventory	4,000
Current liability adjustments	
Add: Increase in accounts payable	8,000
Less: Decrease in salaries payable	(7,000)
Add: Increase in interest payable	1,000
Add: Increase in taxes payable	2,000
Cash flow from operations	**85,000**

© Kaplan, Inc.

103 - 10

Calculating CFI

CFI =

cash received on asset sales - investment in assets

Net book value =

Gross PPE – accumulated depreciation

Gain (loss) on sale = sales price – net book value

© Kaplan, Inc.

104

Ecclestone CFI

Calculating NBV of asset sold

Gross Plant and Equip.		Accumulated Depr.	
Beginning PPE	282,000	Begin Acc. Depr.	80,000
Additions	50,000	Depr. Expense	14,000
PPE disposal	(20,000)	AD for disposal	(10,000)
Ending PPE	312,000	End Acc. Depr.	84,000

NBV of disposal = 20,000 – 10,000 = **10,000**

© Kaplan, Inc.

105 - 6

Ecclestone CFI

CFI = cash additions – cash received on disposal

	$
Sale Proceeds	30,000
– NBV of disposal	10,000
Gain (loss) on sale	20,000

CFI = –additions + proceeds

CFI = –$50,000 + $30,000 = –$20,000

© Kaplan, Inc.

106 - 3

Last year Acme Corp. bought an asset for $72,000, depreciation expense was $15,000, accumulated depreciation increased by $5,000, and gross PPE increased by $32,000. If a gain on an asset sold during the year was $13,000, the sales proceeds on the asset sale were:

A. $30,000.

B. $43,000.

C. $48,000.

© Kaplan, Inc.

107 - 5

Slide 108

Computing CFF

- C ange in debt
- Change in common stock
- Cash dividends paid

$$\$$$

Net income	X	Dividends declared	(X)
Dividends declared	(X)	ΔDividends payable	X
Δ in retained earnings	X	Cash paid	(X)

© Kaplan, Inc.

108

Slide 109-9

Ecclestone CFF

$$\$$$

- Change in debt   10,000
- Change in common stock   (20,000)
- Cash dividends paid   (7,000)
                                            (17,000)

$$\$$$

Net income	75,000	Dividends decl.	(17,000)
Div declared	(17,000)	Δ Div. payable	10,000
Δ in R/E	58,000	Cash div. paid	(7,000)

© Kaplan, Inc.

109 - 9

Slide 110-3

Putting the Cash Flow Statement Together

	$
Cash flow from operations	85,000
Cash flow from investments	(20,000)
Cash flow from financing	(17,000)
Net increase in cash	48,000
Cash balance 12/31/X8	18,000
Cash balance 12/31/X9	66,000

© Kaplan, Inc.

110 - 3

Slide 111

Converting an Indirect Statement to a Direct Statement of Cash Flows

Most firms use the indirect method, but the analyst may want information on the cash flows by function; some examples of this technique are:

Net sales – Δ accounts receivable + Δ advances from customers = cash collections

Cost of goods sold + Δ inventory – Δ accounts payable = cash paid for inputs (**COGS treated as positive number**)

Interest expense + Δ interest payable = cash interest

© Kaplan, Inc.

111

Slide 112

Direct Method From Indirect CFO

1. Take each income statement item in turn (e.g., sales)

2. Move to the balance sheet and identify asset and liability accounts that relate to that income statement item—e.g., accounts receivable

3. Calculate the change in the balance sheet item during the period (ending balance – opening balance)

4. Apply the rule:

> Increases in an asset: deduct
> Increase in a liability: add
> Decrease in an asset: add
> Decrease in a liability: deduct

© Kaplan, Inc.

112

Slide 113

Direct From Indirect CFO

5. Adjust the income statement amount by the change in the balance sheet

6. Tick off the items dealt with in both the income statement and balance sheet

7. Move to the next item on the income statement and repeat

8. Ignore depreciation/amortization and gains/losses on the disposal of assets as these are non-cash or non-CFO items

© Kaplan, Inc.

113

Slide 114

Direct From Indirect CFO

9. Keep moving down the income statement until all items included in net income have been addressed applying steps 1-8

10. Total up the amounts and you have CFO

© Kaplan, Inc.

114

Slide 115

Direct From Indirect CFO

Cash Inflows

Sales	200,000	
Less: Increase in A/R	(2,000)	
Cash collected from customers		198,000

Direct cash outflows

Cost of goods sold	(80,000)	
Add: Decrease in inventory	4,000	
Purchases	(76,000)	
Add: Increase in A/P	8,000	
Cash paid to suppliers		(68,000)

Operating expense (wages)	(10,000)	
Less: Decrease in salaries payable	(7,000)	
Cash paid to employees		(17,000)

© Kaplan, Inc.

115 - 6

LOS 27.g Convert
CFAI p. 293, Schweser p. 121

Understanding Cash Flow
Statements

Direct From Indirect CFO (continued)

	$	$
Cash outflows		
Interest Expense	(1,000)	
Add: Increase in interest payable	1,000	
Cash interest paid		0
Tax Expense	(40,000)	
Add: Increase in deferred tax liab.	10,000	
Tax payable	(30,000)	
Add: Increase in taxes payable	2,000	
Cash taxes paid		(28,000)
	CFO	85,000

© Kaplan, Inc.

116 - 6

LOS 27.h Analyze/Interpret
CFAI p. 294, Schweser p. 124

Understanding Cash Flow
Statements

Cash Flow Statement Analysis

Do regular operations generate enough cash to sustain the business?

Is enough cash is generated to pay off maturing debt?

Highlights the need for additional finance

Ability to meet unexpected obligations

The flexibility to take advantage of new business opportunities

Benefits for the analyst

© Kaplan, Inc.

117

LOS 27.h Analyze/Interpret
CFAI p. 294, Schweser p. 124

Understanding Cash Flow
Statements

Analysis

1. Analyze the major sources and uses of cash flow (CFO, CFI, CFF)
   - Where are the major sources and uses?
   - Is CFO positive and sufficient to cover capex?

2. Analyze CFO
   - What are the major determinants of CFO?
   - Is CFO higher or lower than NI?
   - How consistent is CFO?

© Kaplan, Inc.

118

LOS 27.h Analyze/Interpret
CFAI p. 294, Schweser p. 124

Understanding Cash Flow
Statements

Analysis

3. Analyze CFI
   - What is cash being spent on?
   - Is the company investing in PP&E?
   - What acquisitions have been made?

4. Analyze CFF
   - How is the company financing CFI and CFO?
   - Is the company raising or repaying capital?
   - What dividends are being returned to owners?

© Kaplan, Inc.

119

Slide 120

Common Size Statements

Two Approaches

Show each item as a % of net revenue

Show each inflow as a % of total inflows

Show each outflow as a % of total outflows

Useful for:

Forecasting future cash flows (% of net revenue)

Useful for:

Trend analysis (time series)

© Kaplan, Inc.

120

Slide 121

Common Size Statements Ecclestone

Inflows

Receipts from customers	$198,000	83.2%
Sale of equipment	$30,000	12.6%
Debt issuance	$10,000	4.2%
Total	$238,000	100%

© Kaplan, Inc.

121

Slide 122

Common Size Statements Ecclestone

Outflows

Payments to suppliers	$68,000	35.8%
Payments to employees	$17,000	8.9%
Payments for interest	$0	0%
Payments for income tax	$28,000	14.7%
Purchase of equipment	$50,000	26.3%
Retirement of common stock	$20,000	10.5%
Dividend payments	$7,000	3.7%
Total	$190,000	100%

© Kaplan, Inc.

122

Slide 123

Free Cash Flow (FCF)

- FCF is cash available for discretionary uses

- Frequently used to value firms

- $FCFF = NI + NCC - WCInv + Int (1-T) - FCInv$

- $FCFF = CFO + Int (1-T) - FCInv$

- $FCFE = CFO - FCInv + Net\ debt\ increase$

© Kaplan, Inc.

123

Free Cash Flow (FCF) Ecclestone

- $FCFF = CFO + Int(1-T) - FCInv$

  $\$85,000 + \$1,000 (1-0.4) - \$20,000 = \$65,600$

- $FCFE = CFO - FCInv + Net\ debt\ increase$

  $\$85,000 - \$20,000 + \$10,000 = \$75,000$

- $FCFE = FCFF - Int(1-T) + Net\ debt\ increase$

  $\$65,600 - \$1,000 (1-0.4) + \$10,000 = \$75,000$

124 - 3

Cash Flow Performance Ratios

Cash flow to revenue

$$\frac{CFO}{Net\ revenue}$$

Cash return on assets

$$\frac{CFO}{Avg\ total\ assets}$$

Cash return on equity

$$\frac{CFO}{Avg\ equity}$$

Cash to income

$$\frac{CFO}{Operating\ income}$$

125

Cash Flow Performance Ratios

Cash flow per share*

$$\frac{CFO - pref\ div}{\#\ common\ stock}$$

*IFRS: If dividends paid
were treated as CFO, they
must be added back

126

Cash Flow Coverage Ratios

Debt coverage

$$\frac{CFO}{Total\ debt}$$

Interest coverage*

$$\frac{CFO + interest + tax}{Interest\ paid}$$

Reinvestment

$$\frac{CFO}{Cash\ paid\ for\ long\text{-}term\ assets}$$

*IFRS: If interest paid was
treated as CFF, no addition
is required

127

Slide (top left)

Income Statements, Balance Sheets, and Cash Flow Statements

28. Financial Analysis Techniques

KAPLAN UNIVERSITY | SCHOOL OF PROFESSIONAL AND CONTINUING EDUCATION | SCHWESER

Slide 128 (bottom left)

LOS 27.i Calculate/Interpret
CFAI p. 302, Schweser p. 126

Cash Flow Coverage Ratios

Debt payment

$$\frac{CFO}{\text{Cash paid for long-term debt repayment}}$$

Dividend payment

$$\frac{CFO}{\text{Dividends paid}}$$

Investing and financing

$$\frac{CFO}{\text{Cash outflows for CFI \& CFF}}$$

© Kaplan, Inc.

128

Slide 131 (top right)

LOS 28.a Describe
CFAI p. 318, Schweser p. 142

Vertical Common-Size Statements

Income Statement

$$\frac{\text{Income statement account}}{\text{Sales}} \quad \text{e.g.,} \quad \frac{\text{Marketing expense}}{\text{Sales}}$$

Balance Sheet

$$\frac{\text{Balance sheet account}}{\text{Total assets}} \quad \text{e.g.,} \quad \frac{\text{Inventory}}{\text{Total assets}}$$

© Kaplan, Inc.

131

Slide 130 (bottom right)

LOS 28.a Describe
CFAI p. 318, Schweser p. 142

Interpreting Ratios

1. **Cross-sectional** analysis:

   Comparison to industry norm or average

2. **Time-series** analysis (trend analysis):

   Comparison to a company's past ratios

Ratios help the analyst identify the questions that need answering.

© Kaplan, Inc.

130

Common-Size Income Statement

Example: Consider a common-size income statement that reveals the following (selected items only):

Income Statement Item	20X7	20X8	Industry Avg.
COGS	58%	62%	60%
SG&A	18%	22%	18%
Net Income	9%	8%	10%

© Kaplan, Inc.   133

Categories of Ratios

- **Activity**   →   Efficiency of day-to-day tasks/operations

- **Liquidity**   →   Ability to meet short-term liabilities

- **Solvency**   →   Ability to meet long-term obligations

- **Profitability** →   Ability to generate profitable sales from asset base

- **Valuation**   →   Quantity of asset or flow associated with an ownership claim

© Kaplan, Inc.   135

Horizontal Common-Size Statements

- Each line shown as a relative to some base year
- Facilitates trend analysis

Assets	Year 0	Year 1	Year 2
Cash	1.0	1.2	1.1
AR	1.0	1.3	1.0
Inventory	1.0	0.8	1.2
PP&E	1.0	1.5	2.0
Total	1.0	1.3	1.5

© Kaplan, Inc.   132

Limitations of Financial Ratios

- **Not useful in isolation** – only valid when compared to other firms or the company's historical performance

- **Different accounting treatments** – particularly when analyzing non-U.S. firms

- **Finding comparable industry ratios** for companies that operate in multiple industries (homogeneity of operating activities)

- All ratios must be viewed **relative** to one another

- Determining the target or comparison value requires some **range of acceptable values**

© Kaplan, Inc.   134

Ratio Analysis Context

1. Company goals and strategy

2. Industry norms
   - Ratios may be **industry specific**
   - **Multiple lines** of business distort aggregate ratios
   - Differences in **accounting methods**

3. Economic conditions
   - Cyclical businesses and the **stage of the business cycle**

© Kaplan, Inc.

136

Ratio Analysis

Some general rules:

- For ratios that use only **income statement items**, use the values from the current income statement.

- For ratios using only **balance sheet items**, use the values from the current balance sheet.

- For ratios using **both income statement and balance sheet items**, use the value from the current income statement and the **average value for the balance sheet item.**

© Kaplan, Inc.

137

Activity Ratios

$$\text{Inventory turnover} = \frac{\text{Cost of goods sold}}{\text{Average inventory}}$$

$$\text{Days of inventory on hand (DOH)} = \frac{365}{\text{Inventory turnover}}$$

$$\text{Receivables turnover} = \frac{\text{Revenue}}{\text{Average receivables}}$$

$$\text{Days of sales outstanding (DSO)} = \frac{365}{\text{Receivables turnover}}$$

© Kaplan, Inc.

138

Activity Ratios

$$\text{Payables turnover} = \frac{\text{Purchases}}{\text{Average trade payables}}$$

$$\text{Number of days of payables} = \frac{365}{\text{Payables turnover}}$$

$$\text{Working capital turnover} = \frac{\text{Revenue}}{\text{Average working capital}}$$

$$\text{Working capital} = \text{Current assets} - \text{Current liabilities}$$

© Kaplan, Inc.

139

Slide 140 — Activity Ratios

Activity Ratios

$$\text{Fixed asset turnover} = \frac{\text{Revenue}}{\text{Average net fixed assets}}$$

Net of accumulated depreciation

$$\text{Total asset turnover} = \frac{\text{Revenue}}{\text{Average total assets}}$$

© Kaplan, Inc.   140

Slide 141 — Definitions: Liquidity Ratios

Definitions: Liquidity Ratios

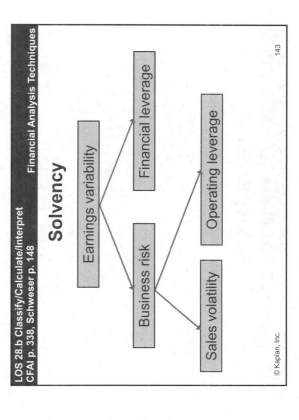

$$\text{Defensive interval ratio} = \frac{\text{Cash + short-term marketable investments + receivables}}{\text{Daily cash expenditure}}$$

	Days
DOH	X
DSO	X
No. of days of payables	(X)
Cash conversion cycle	X

Cash conversion cycle =

© Kaplan, Inc.   141

Slide 142–4 — Cash Conversion Cycle

Cash Conversion Cycle

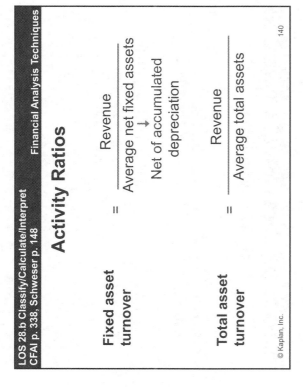

© Kaplan, Inc.   142 – 4

Slide 143 — Solvency

Solvency

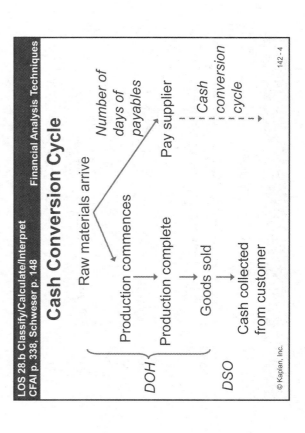

© Kaplan, Inc.   143

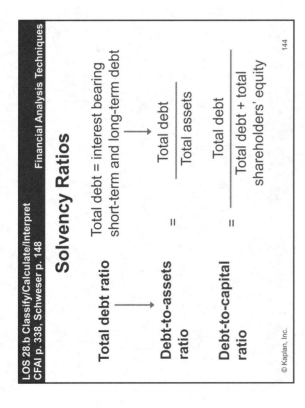

Slide 144

Solvency Ratios

Total debt ratio → Total debt = interest bearing short-term and long-term debt

Debt-to-assets ratio $= \dfrac{\text{Total debt}}{\text{Total assets}}$

Debt-to-capital ratio $= \dfrac{\text{Total debt}}{\text{Total debt + total shareholders' equity}}$

© Kaplan, Inc.

144

Slide 145

Solvency Ratios

Debt-to-equity ratio $= \dfrac{\text{Total debt}}{\text{Total shareholders' equity}}$

Financial leverage ratio $= \dfrac{\text{Average total assets}}{\text{Average total equity}}$

© Kaplan, Inc.

145

Slide 146

Solvency Ratios

Interest coverage $= \dfrac{\text{EBIT}}{\text{Interest payments}}$

Fixed charge coverage $= \dfrac{\text{EBIT + lease payments}}{\text{Interest payments + lease payments}}$

© Kaplan, Inc.

146

Slide 147

Profitability Ratios

Return on assets (ROA) $= \dfrac{\text{Net income}}{\text{Average total assets}}$

Alternatively:
Return on assets (ROA) $= \dfrac{\text{Net income + interest expense }(1 - T)}{\text{Average total assets}}$

Operating ROA $= \dfrac{\text{Operating income}}{\text{Average total assets}}$

© Kaplan, Inc.

147

LOS 28.b Classify/Calculate/Interpret
CFAI p. 338, Schweser p. 148   Financial Analysis Techniques

Profitability Ratios

Return on total
capital

$$= \frac{EBIT}{\text{Short- + long-term debt} + \text{equity}}$$

Return on equity
(ROE)

$$= \frac{\text{Net income}}{\text{Average total equity}}$$

Return on
common equity

$$= \frac{\text{Net income} - \text{pref. div.}}{\text{Average common equity}}$$

© Kaplan, Inc.   148

LOS 28.c Describe/Evaluate
CFAI p. 359, Schweser p. 157   Financial Analysis Techniques

Integrated Financial Ratio Approach

- Important to **analyze** all ratios **collectively**

- Use information from one ratio category to
  answer questions raised by another ratio

  - Classic example = DuPont analysis

© Kaplan, Inc.   149

LOS 28.c Describe/Evaluate
CFAI p. 359, Schweser p. 157   Financial Analysis Techniques

Integrated Financial Ratios – Example

	20X8	20X7	20X6
Current ratio	2.0	1.5	1.2
Quick ratio	0.5	0.8	1.0
	20X8	20X7	20X6
DOH	60	50	30
DSO	20	30	40

What can you conclude about this firm's performance?
(Note that years are presented right-to-left.)

© Kaplan, Inc.   150

LOS 28.c Describe/Evaluate
CFAI p. 359, Schweser p. 157   Financial Analysis Techniques

Integrated Financial Ratios – Example

1. Current ratio up – Quick ratio down – Why?

2. DOH has increased – indicates rising
   inventory rather than low cash

3. DSO decreasing – collecting cash from
   customers sooner

4. Current and quick ratios indicate the
   collected cash is being spent on inventory
   accumulation

5. Appears collections have been accelerated
   to make up for poor inventory management

© Kaplan, Inc.   151 - 5

LOS 28.d Demonstrate/Calculate/Interpret   Financial Analysis Techniques
CFAI p. 361, Schweser p. 162

DuPont System Analysis

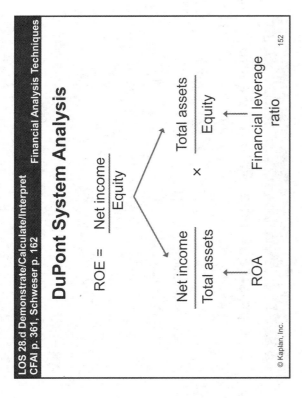

152

LOS 28.d Demonstrate/Calculate/Interpret   Financial Analysis Techniques
CFAI p. 361, Schweser p. 162

DuPont System: Original Equation

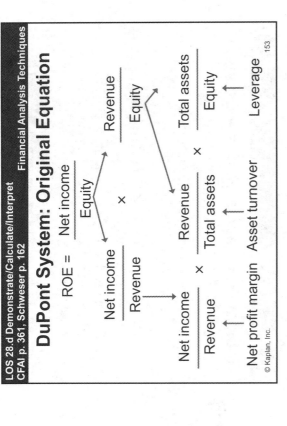

153

LOS 28.d Demonstrate/Calculate/Interpret   Financial Analysis Techniques
CFAI p. 361, Schweser p. 162

DuPont System: Extended Equation

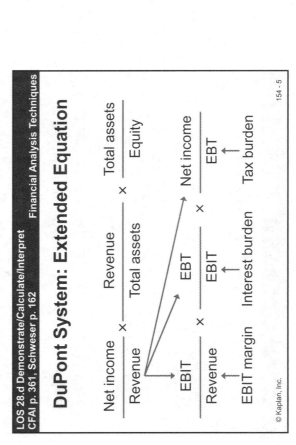

154 - 5

LOS 28.d Demonstrate/Calculate/Interpret   Financial Analysis Techniques
CFAI p. 361, Schweser p. 162

DuPont System: Extended Equation

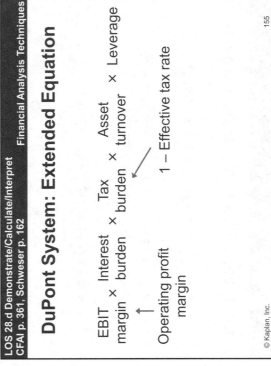

155

Per-Share Ratios for Valuation

$$\frac{P}{E} = \frac{\text{Price per share}}{\text{Earnings per share}}$$

$$\frac{P}{CF} = \frac{\text{Price per share}}{\text{Cash flow per share}}$$

$$\frac{P}{S} = \frac{\text{Price per share}}{\text{Sales per share}}$$

$$\frac{P}{BV} = \frac{\text{Price per Share}}{\text{Book value per share}}$$

© Kaplan, Inc.   156

Per-Share Quantities

$$\text{Basic EPS} = \frac{\text{NI} - \text{Pref. div.}}{\text{Weighted avg. \# ordinary shares}}$$

$$\text{Diluted EPS} = \frac{\text{Income adjusted for dilutive securities}}{\text{Weighted avg. \# shares adjusted for dilution}}$$

$$\text{Cash flow per share} = \frac{\text{CFO}}{\text{Weighted avg. \# shares}}$$

© Kaplan, Inc.   157

Per-Share Quantities

$$\text{EBITDA per share} = \frac{\text{EBITDA}}{\text{Avg. \# ordinary shares}}$$

$$\text{Dividends per share} = \frac{\text{Common dividend}}{\text{Weighted avg. \# common shares}}$$

© Kaplan, Inc.   158

Dividend Related Quantities

$$\text{Dividend payout ratio} = \frac{\text{Common dividend}}{\text{Net income} - \text{pref div}} \rightarrow \text{Net income attributable to common shares}$$

$$\text{Retention rate } (b) = \frac{\text{Net income attributable to common shares} - \text{common dividend}}{\text{Net income attributable to common shares}}$$

© Kaplan, Inc.   159

LOS 28.e Calculate/Interpret
CFAI p. 366, Schweser p. 166

Financial Analysis Techniques

Dividend Related Quantities

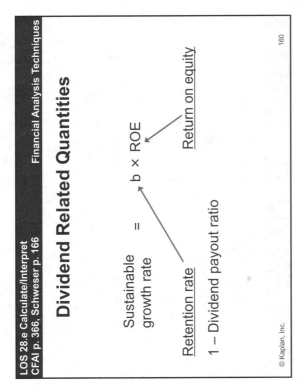

$$\text{Sustainable growth rate} = b \times \text{ROE}$$

Return on equity

Retention rate

1 − Dividend payout ratio

© Kaplan, Inc.

160

LOS 28.e Calculate/Interpret
CFAI p. 366, Schweser p. 166

Financial Analysis Techniques

A firm has a dividend payout ratio of 35%, a net profit margin of 10%, an asset turnover of 1.4, and an equity multiplier leverage measure of 1.2. Estimate the firm's sustainable growth rate.

© Kaplan, Inc.

161 - 4

LOS 28.e Calculate/Interpret
CFAI p. 366, Schweser p. 166

Financial Analysis Techniques

Business Risk Ratios

Coefficient of variation of operating income $= \dfrac{\text{Std. dev. operating income}}{\text{Mean operating income}}$

Coefficient of variation of net income $= \dfrac{\text{Std. dev. net income}}{\text{Mean net income}}$

Coefficient of variation of revenue $= \dfrac{\text{Std. dev. revenue}}{\text{Mean revenue}}$

© Kaplan, Inc.

162

LOS 28.e Calculate/Interpret
CFAI p. 366, Schweser p. 166

Financial Analysis Techniques

Using Ratios for Equity Analysis

Research has found ratios (and changes in ratios) can be useful in forecasting earnings and stock returns (valuation).

Some items useful in forecasting:

% change in: current ratio • quick ratio • inventory • inventory turnover • inventory/total assets • sales • depreciation • capex/assets • asset turnover • depreciation/plant assets • total assets

ROE • Δ ROE • debt/equity • ROA • gross margin • working capital/assets • dividends/cash flow • Δ dividend • % debt repaid • operating ROA • pretax margin

© Kaplan, Inc.

163

LOS 28.e Calculate/Interpret
CFAI p. 366, Schweser p. 166   **Financial Analysis Techniques**

Credit Ratings and Ratios

Assessing a company's ability to service and repay its debt:

Interest coverage ratios | Also covered in
Return on capital | Fixed Income
Debt-to-assets ratio
Other ratios focus on various measures of cash flow to total debt

Note: Adjustments are made for off-balance-sheet debt

© Kaplan, Inc.   164

LOS 28.f Explain/Calculate/Interpret
CFAI p. 375, Schweser p. 170   **Financial Analysis Techniques**

Segment Reporting

Reportable business or geographic segment:
50% of its revenue from sales external to the firm, **and** at least 10% of a firm's revenue, earnings, or assets

- For each segment, firm reports *limited* financial statement information.
  - For primary segments, must report revenue (internal and external), operating profit, assets, liabilities (IFRS only), capex, depreciation, and amortization.

© Kaplan, Inc.   165

LOS 28.f Explain/Calculate/Interpret
CFAI p. 375, Schweser p. 170   **Financial Analysis Techniques**

Definitions: Segment Ratios

$$\text{Segment (net) margin} = \frac{\text{Segment profit}}{\text{Segment revenue}}$$

$$\text{Segment asset turnover} = \frac{\text{Segment revenue}}{\text{Segment assets}}$$

$$\text{Segment ROA} = \frac{\text{Segment profit}}{\text{Segment assets}}$$

$$\text{Segment debt ratio (IFRS only)} = \frac{\text{Segment liabilities}}{\text{Segment assets}}$$

© Kaplan, Inc.   166

LOS 28.g Describe
CFAI p. 378, Schweser p. 171   **Financial Analysis Techniques**

Model Building

- Common-size statements and ratios can be used to model/forecast results
  - Expected relationships among financial statement data
  - Earnings model
  - Revenue driven models
- Sensitivity analysis
- Scenario analysis
- Simulation

© Kaplan, Inc.   167

Financial Analysis Techniques

Analysis has generated the following data:

Tax rate	35%
Equity multiplier	2.7
Net profit margin	4.6%
Equity turnover	5.2

ROE is *closest* to:

A. 13%

B. 17%

C. 24%

168 - 3

STUDY SESSION 8 ANSWERS

Reading	Slide Number	Answer
25	24	B
25	55	C
27	107	B
28	161	10.92%
28	168	C

Notes